Getting the Buggers to Write

D1464373

Also by Sue Cowley:

Getting the Buggers into Drama
Getting the Buggers to Behave, fourth edition
Getting the Buggers to Think, second edition
Getting your Little Darlings to Behave
Guerilla Guide to Teaching, second edition
How to Survive Your First Year in Teaching, second
    edition
Letting the Buggers be Creative
Sue Cowley's A–Z of Teaching
Sue Cowley's Teaching Clinic

Getting the Buggers to Write

Third edition

SUE COWLEY

continuum

A companion website to accompany this book is available online at:
http://education.cowley2.continuumbooks.com

Please type in the URL above and receive your unique password for access to the book's online resources.

If you experience any problems accessing the resources, please contact Continuum at: info@continuumbooks.com

Continuum International Publishing Group

The Tower Building	80 Maiden Lane
11 York Road	Suite 704
London	New York
SE1 7NX	NY 10038

www.continuumbooks.com

© Sue Cowley 2011

British Library Cataloguing-in-Publication Data
A catalogue record for this book is available from the British Library.

ISBN: 978-1-4411-7130-6 (paperback)

Library of Congress Cataloging-in-Publication Data
Cowley, Sue.
Getting the buggers to write / Sue Cowley. -- 3rd ed.
p. cm.
Includes index.
ISBN 978-1-4411-7130-6 -- ISBN 978-1-4411-4332-7 -- ISBN 978-1-4411-9349-0 1. English language--Composition and exercises--Study and teaching (Elementary)--Great Britain. 2. English language--Composition and exercises--Study and teaching (Secondary)--Great Britain. I. Title.

LB1576.C7525 2011
372.62'3--dc22   2011010086

Typeset by Saxon Graphics Ltd, Derby DE21 4SZ
Printed and bound in India

This book is dedicated to Álvie and Edite Castellino, with all my love. I hope you both grow up to love writing as much as I do.

Contents

Contents

Contents

Author's Note, Third Edition

Before we begin, I have a confession to make. I might call myself 'a writer' or if I'm feeling fancy 'an author', but what I actually do is talk to people. That's what I'm doing to you right now. Yes, the words are written down and printed out on a page (or, increasingly likely these days, residing on a screen of some kind), but in essence I'm talking to you through the medium of the written word. And what I most need to happen is for you to feel that, as you read this book, you can hear my voice inside your head: enthusing, warning, suggesting, urging, advising, and hopefully inspiring too.

If you take a quick look around your classroom, you'll find it easy to identify those students who can write well, and equally those ones who struggle. What you're actually considering, though, is who can express themselves through language, who is good at articulating what they want to say? Yes, the nuts and bolts matter – they've got to be able to form letters, words and sentences, to spell, to punctuate, to paragraph. But even when every single one of those aspects is perfectly in place, they must still have that desire to communicate, to express themselves, before you can hope to get quality writing out of them.

As we move ever further into the 'digital age', there are more and more ways in which our students can satisfy an urge to communicate. As teachers we have a duty to give them the tools with which to express themselves. Equally, we have a duty to inspire them to use the medium of language to get their thoughts, ideas, creative expression, opinions – whatever they wish! – out into the world. Because it's only when they can connect with an audience of readers that their writing really comes to life.

Please note that this is most definitely not a book about meeting targets or getting to grips with the latest government strategies for literacy. Nor is it a book about working out how to (in that awful phrase which makes being a teacher sound like working for a courier company) 'deliver the curriculum'. In education, fads and fashions come and go, governments and education departments change, vast forests of trees are wasted in bringing you the very latest initiatives. But when it comes to what actually happens in the classroom, good quality, inspirational teaching remains pretty much constant. And that's what this book is about.

I'm hugely fortunate to write professionally. And when I think back to my own education, I owe a vote of thanks to those teachers who helped me learn how to write, and who inspired in me the desire to communicate my thoughts and ideas. It's my hope that the third edition of this book will help you get your students to become excellent writers. By equipping them to write well, you give them the best chance to succeed in life, to grasp all the opportunities they have to express themselves, and to contribute their ideas and thoughts to the world in whatever form they choose. It's a big challenge, but equally a huge honour. I wish you well in your quest.

Sue Cowley
www.suecowley.co.uk

Acknowledgements

Thanks to all the brilliant English teachers who have taught me, worked with me and inspired me, especially Miss Ladd, Hilary, Valerie and the three Johns. Thanks to Anthony Haynes for the title, and to Alexandra Webster as well – you've moved on, but you're not forgotten! Thanks to Melanie Wilson and Rosie Pattinson at Continuum. And, of course, thanks as always to Tilak.

Introduction

The pen is the tongue of the mind.

Miguel de Cervantes

The written word is all around us: the form varies, the language changes with time, but the impulse to communicate through writing is a constant. For those of us who work in education, writing is fundamental. Every subject taught in schools and colleges demands that, at some point, the student must pick up a pen and make marks on paper. Or, as we march ever onwards into the digital age, that they should type their thoughts on-screen. How, then, can we 'kick-start' the writing process, whether this means getting young children confident about using the written word, or fighting the disaffection that some older students feel? How can we motivate and inspire our students to write, especially those for whom writing is a real struggle? And once we've got them motivated, how can we ensure that the writing they produce is clear, accurate, well written and enjoyable?

This book aims to answer these questions. The ideas here will be of most interest to English teachers, and to those staff working to improve literacy in primary schools. But equally there should be much food for thought here for those helping students to write in all areas of the curriculum. Whatever part of the sector you work in, and whatever subject you teach, remember that we *all* have a stake in improving our students' literacy skills and their motivation to express themselves through language.

In this book you will find a combination of tips, teaching strategies, examples and exercises, from which you can choose those best suited to your particular needs. My hope is that the material here will inspire you to find new and exciting ways to encourage your students to develop their writing. My own experiences as a teacher have taught me that it is often the unusual ideas and strategies that prove effective, especially when working with poorly motivated students.

My primary aim in this book is to offer you *practical* advice, written in an honest, accessible and straightforward way – advice that will be of immediate use to you in the classroom or setting in which you work. The ideas included in this book are based on my own experiences as a teacher and as a writer. I have tried to avoid jargon and complicated terminology, for these are the enemies of the teacher, and of the writer. When we're communicating, we should always try to put across what we want to say as simply and clearly as possible. There's nothing clever about using big words and confusing acronyms for their own sake. Every word must serve a purpose.

In recent years there's been a strong focus on the importance of literacy and the skills and experiences that children need to help them communicate effectively. What this means is that teachers in all subject areas are becoming ever more aware of how crucial (and complex) the acquisition of literacy actually is. Within this book, you will find strategies and approaches to help you teach writing in a way that will motivate and engage all your students, and allow you to give them access to the wonderful gift of literacy.

We write for a multitude of reasons and purposes. Some students write only because they have to, because Miss or Sir is leaning on their shoulders and threatening all manner of consequences if they refuse to put pen to paper. Other students genuinely enjoy the chance to express themselves through words. The majority of our students are involved in written communication every day of their lives, although they might not realize it, or consider it to be 'writing'. Outside of class time (and sometimes even during lessons!), the sound of text messages being sent and received has become the new soundtrack of our school days. Emails, chat-rooms and social networking sites have become the digital equivalent of the paper messages that we used to pass around amongst our peers.

The reality for teachers in the classroom starts with motivating students to turn their thoughts into words, and to present these on paper. We need to show them that writing is important, and make it clear that there is no hidden secret to good writing, simply a range of techniques that we have to learn. Writing well is about learning the skills (and tricks) that help create good writing. Just as a violin player must learn musical technique before adding the expression that brings his or her playing to life, so we must teach our pupils the techniques that writing involves, and help them learn how to express themselves in an accurate and imaginative way.

 You'll see, scattered through this book, a symbol that looks like the one in the margin. Wherever you see this symbol, go to the companion website to find useful links, downloadable resources and texts for you to use in class. You can also find additional writing resources, and a place to publish your own and your students' writing, at my website: www.cele-brate-writing.co.uk.

It is my hope that the third edition of this book will help you get your students writing, and writing as well as they possibly can. If I'm honest, I also hope that this book will inspire you to write more yourself. Celebrate writing, in all its forms and in all its wonderful complexity. Throw open your mind, and share what is in there through the magical medium of words.

Sue Cowley
www.celebrate-writing.co.uk

Please note: to keep things simple, I have used a mixture of 'he' and 'she' throughout this book when talking about students.

Part 1

Starting Points

1

First Steps to Writing

A journey of a thousand miles starts with a single step.

Confucius

The journey to literacy, and to becoming a writer, is a long, hard and complex one. I'm very lucky in that I originally trained as an early years teacher, before becoming a secondary English teacher – it gave me an understanding of the first steps in the process of learning to write. Understanding how those 'first steps' happen is illuminating – especially if you're working with older students who seem totally blocked when it comes to expressing themselves through writing. Perhaps your students have gone astray, and are struggling to get back on track; maybe they have special needs such as dyslexia, which have severely delayed their writing; maybe they've been let down by poor teaching or been in a school where poor behaviour stopped them from progressing? In this chapter I show how these early steps can link to writing skills and activities used later on in a student's school career.

Becoming a writer is obviously about learning the letters, but it's also about acquiring a set of physical, intellectual and emotional skills and attitudes that go together to make a 'writer'. To be a confident, fluent writer, your students need:

- ✓ an understanding of when and why they might need or want to write
- ✓ a desire to communicate their ideas through writing
- ✓ the confidence to believe that what they say matters
- ✓ the resilience to keep going when it's hard work
- ✓ to have moved from forming letters, to words, to sentences, to paragraphs and then longer pieces of text
- ✓ engaging and inspiring resources with which to express themselves.

The strands of literacy

Although this book is essentially about teaching writing, writing is of course inextricably linked to both reading and to speaking and listening. For the writer, words are what matter, whether they are in your mouth, in someone else's mouth, on a page of a book, on a computer screen, or being made by a pen.

Reading and writing: the vital link

There is a crucial link between the dual literacy skills of reading and writing. Reading feeds into writing: not least because if a reader sees a letter or word frequently, they are more likely to be able to remember and replicate its shape (it's not *all* about sound). Reading also feeds into writing because it helps our students understand what writing is for: that books and other texts are a source of pleasure, education, information, and so on. This is not a book about teaching students to read, but if you want your students to become good writers, you must encourage them to read as frequently and as widely as possible. Present them with different kinds of writing, and read to them from a range of texts (yes, stories, but also non fiction, poetry, posters, computers, and so on). By doing this, you will help them become more effective writers.

Teachers can encourage lots of reading by:

✓ involving parents or carers whenever possible
✓ getting students reading anything and everything
✓ making sure there's a clear reason for reading
✓ showing students that texts and reading are a natural part of life
✓ teaching students to read as a writer and write as a reader
✓ showing them that you're a reader/writer too.

Speaking/listening and writing: the weakest link?

At its heart, all writing is about communication. When I write, I type down the words that I would speak to an audience of educators (obviously with some editing to make the text clear, concise and hopefully engaging). Writing is effectively about speaking to your reader via the written word. This link between speaking and writing means that students who find it hard to listen to others, or to articulate themselves in speech, will have problems doing the same in writing. If a student finds it hard to construct short, concise and clear phrases or sentences verbally, then this weakness will inevitably be transmitted to the page. Students will typically write as they speak – 'would of' instead of 'would have' or 'would've'.

To develop your students' skills, practise speaking and listening in a range of formats. Aim to:

- ✓ build their confidence
- ✓ make activities fun and engaging
- ✓ set lots of challenges
- ✓ talk about how speech is structured
- ✓ identify formal and informal language
- ✓ develop the use of Standard English
- ✓ use lots of different listening tasks
- ✓ teach good listening behaviour.

Early mark making

From a very early age (often before they are even two) children start to make marks. The urge to draw and write seems hard-wired into our genetic make-up – as soon as our hands are big and strong enough to hold a writing implement, we can hardly wait to get going. There is a certain magic about the very earliest part of the process of learning to write – what is known in early years as 'mark making'. At this stage, the emphasis is on motivating and inspiring children to make those marks – through painting, colouring, mucky play – and helping them develop the fine motor skills required to hold a writing tool.

In the early years children are given access to a wide range of resources to inspire their mark making. There's no harm at all in offering some of these same resources to much older students, to reinvigorate them and to release their creative energies. Indeed, if you're working with students who have a special need such as dyslexia or autism, many of these approaches are acknowledged as good practice. Have a think about how you might utilize some of these ideas with your own students.

What could the students write with? Pens, pencils, crayons, whiteboard markers, chalks and charcoals, outdoor chalks, paint, mud, wool trailed in paint.

What could the students write on? Plain paper – small sheets, huge scale, graph paper, clipboards, mini-whiteboards, Post-its, envelopes, postcards.

What could the students write in? Sand, water, the air, clay, ice, wax.

9

What could the students make letter shapes with? Plasticine, vegetables, dough, their fingers, bodies, shadows, pipe cleaners.

Where could the students do their writing? Indoors, outdoors, on large sheets of paper pinned on a wall, directly onto a specific wall outside, on the ground (tarmac, earth, pavement), under a table, during a drama activity, in a forest, during a walk.

What kind of inspirations can I use for writing? A shopping list, a menu at a café, a pizza recipe, a postcard from an alien, writing cards (Christmas, birthday), treasure hunts.

Early writing techniques

It might seem odd to be talking about writing techniques in the early stages of learning to write. However, this is the stage at which certain key techniques must be learned. Students very easily get into the wrong habits around writing, for instance holding a pencil in the wrong way, or forming letters incorrectly. It's far easier and better to get into the right habit from the start, than for the student to have to unlearn a bad habit later on. If you're working with older students who have got themselves into bad habits, the process of 'unlearning' these parts of the process can be a real struggle.

When considering technique, make sure that you:

✓ *Get the physical action right:* Are your writers holding their pencils or pens in the correct way, sometimes referred to as a 'tripod grip'? You can find manufactured pen-holders to make this easier for them, or mould Plasticine around a pen to make it easier to grip correctly.
✓ *Experiment with different instruments:* Some students find a chunky pen size easier to work with; others prefer to write with a felt tip rather than a pen or pencil. Experiment to find the instrument that best suits each individual, rather than insisting on a 'one size fits all' approach.
✓ *Consider posture:* Good posture is a key part of a good writing technique. Consider the furniture in your room – is it conducive to good posture? Can you make any practical changes? Encourage your students to sit up tall, with legs uncrossed. Check the table height: students should not have to bend their wrists to reach the surface, nor bend their backs over to write. As students get older, and are

asked to write for longer periods of time, this becomes ever more important.

Finger exercises

One of the key writing techniques is for students to develop the muscles in their fingers. Incorporate activities specifically aimed at developing hand and finger strength. As they get older, and are asked to write more frequently and for longer, these exercises help them avoid muscle fatigue in their fingers and hands.

For instance, you can get them to:

✓ Touch a thumb to each finger in turn (thumb to index, thumb to middle, thumb to ring, thumb to little, then back again). Repeat this exercise with both hands together.
✓ Separate the fingers so that index and middle are together on one side, and ring and little together on the other. Now change so that middle and ring are held together, and the other two fingers are on their own.
✓ Wriggle individual fingers, one at a time.

Find a link to information sheets about prewriting techniques on the companion website.

Letter activities

It's not long before children are ready to move on from mark-making activities, to learning the formation of letters. The key skills at this point are to understand the shapes and sound of each letter, and also to focus on using the correct direction for writing them. Again, you might find yourself working with students who get letter direction or formation confused.

Here are some imaginative and hands-on ideas for reinforcing correct letter formation:

✓ Get your students to draw letters and words in the air with their fingers, focusing on the correct direction in which to write.
✓ Have a 'letter of the day', focusing on commonly mistaken forma-tions such as 'b' and 'd'.
✓ Ask your class to think of words that start with a particular letter sound – who can find the most words that start with this letter?

✓ Sculpt letters out of clay or dough.
✓ Make a collage of images that all start with the same letter of the alphabet.
✓ For the very weak students, use tracing and join the dots activities.

Many of these activities can also be used to help students remember letter blends.

From letters to words

Young children quickly have enough letters, and letter blends, under their belt to start creating words. Now they can start to 'write' – to express themselves through language, although at first this is hesitant. Typically, children are far quicker to read than they are to write. It takes a while for them to gain enough confidence to use language on paper. Of course, they don't have to know the exact spelling of lots of words before they can write to express themselves.

Use these word-level activities for older learners who have English as a second or additional language, or for those who find literacy a real struggle:

✓ Using Scrabble tiles, call out a word and get your students to spell it.
✓ Give students a word that has been jumbled up – what does it say?
✓ Use word searches as an excellent way for students to gain confidence and look for letter patterns.
✓ Introduce parts of language in an active way, for instance getting volunteers to act out verbs for the class.
✓ Talk with your students about the kind of approaches they could use to work out how a word is spelt.

From words to sentences

Once children have mastered a sufficient range of vocabulary, they are ready to start forming sentences. These two processes (learning how to spell words, creating sentences) happen simultaneously. At the most basic level, all that children need to construct a sentence is knowledge of subjects and verbs, so that they can write 'The girl jumps.' At this stage, the complex structures that they are using in their spoken language, and seeing in their reading, will start to translate onto the page. You can find lots of ideas for working on the basic techniques (spelling, punctuation, grammar, etc.) in Chapter 2.

Sentence in my head

In my experience, the most competent writers are generally those who can 'hold' a full sentence in their head, *before* they write it down. They have a sense of the sound and structure of their writing before it goes onto the page: they can 'hear it' in their mind. The most competent writers also have the ability to add tone and expression to that sentence while it is still in their head. Similarly, those older students I've taught who seem totally 'blocked' when it comes to writing, often appear to be unable to use this technique.

If your students find it impossible to 'hold' a full sentence in their head, they can use the same technique but at phrase level. This approach is also great for ensuring that punctuation gets put in the right place – if I've got that whole phrase or sentence 'held' in my head, I know that there will be a comma or full stop at the end of it.

Structure and young writers

One of the key skills of effective writing is to be able to structure a piece of text properly. Of course, students learn how to do this through reading stories, books and other texts, but they also need explicit instruction in how to structure their work. The teacher's role is to help them understand how to do this – by showing them both how to break down pieces of writing into their constituent parts, and how to build up a structure themselves, from the ground upwards.

Using writing frames

For young writers, and less able or less confident older ones, writing frames provide an excellent source of support and inspiration. The framework means they can focus on writing, rather than having to worry about getting the layout correct. You model the way that the frame is used to the class; the students then use the same framework to create their own piece of writing. More able or older students might create a frame for their classmates.

Writing frames are often used for non-fiction pieces, for instance for a:

– newspaper report
– set of instructions

- recipe
- menu
- spell
- letter
- crime scene report.

Aim for a creative focus for your frame – a 'letter to Santa', a 'recipe for the perfect day' – to inspire your students.

Retelling stories

Another excellent approach to teaching structure to young writers is through retelling stories. This also encourages the students to think about how they should sequence their writing. Take a well-known or well-liked story (*The Three Little Pigs, The Very Hungry Caterpillar*). Now, working in groups, ask your students to draw the key or main events in the story in the order that they happen. They can use these pictures as a 'blueprint' to retell the story. Alternatively they could take that original story, and change a few of the elements, for instance creating a tale about a 'very angry alligator'.

What makes a good writer?

Once the technical skills described in this book are in place, everyone should be able to write in at least some form. Whether or not they become a good and effective writer is another matter. Right from the start, it is worth understanding the attributes and attitudes that your students need to develop, in order to write well. The aim should be to encourage these in our students from their very earliest attempts to write. The tips, advice and strategies given throughout this book will help you teach your students to become the best writers that they can possibly be. A good writer, of any age, will be someone who:

✓ talks frequently, fluently and expressively
✓ reads widely and enjoys a variety of texts
✓ loves sharing stories and finding out facts and information
✓ is motivated to communicate via words
✓ is able to concentrate (and sit still) for extended periods of time
✓ has an enjoyment of sounds, words and texts
✓ likes to look at texts, play with them, dig into them to analyse them
✓ reads with an understanding of how the writer works

✓ writes with an awareness of what will work for the reader
✓ has an ability to structure his or her ideas
✓ has an understanding of strategies connected to the technical side of writing
✓ can be both analytical and creative.

The starting points in this chapter show how those youngest writers set off on the journey to becoming confident writers, able to express themselves and their ideas to the full.

2

Building Firm Foundations

The loftier the building, the deeper must the foundation be laid.

Thomas à Kempis

Every piece of writing needs firm foundations – accurate spelling, punctuation and grammar. These are the groundwork that hold the building in place. While students can express themselves without getting the basics completely right, their writing is at its best if it is also technically accurate. This chapter offers you lots of thoughts, ideas and strategies to help you improve your students' grasp of the basics. Traditionally, the job of teaching 'the basics' has taken place during literacy lessons at primary level, or has fallen to English teachers in secondary schools. However, in recent years it's been increasingly acknowledged that teachers in *all* subjects play a part in teaching good writing skills. In this chapter you'll find lots of ideas that could be used with students at different ages, and within various areas of the curriculum.

Back to basics

It's worth considering just why it is so important to get these basic elements right. Share the ideas below with your students. So often we assume that our students know why they are being asked to do something. Make the reasons explicit to increase their understanding and motivation. Pose the question to your students: *why* do you need to be able to write properly? There are many benefits to getting the basics right:

✓ *Confidence*: A firm grasp of the basics allows your students to focus on content and expression. Ideally they should write accurately without having to think about it – for the technique to become subconscious. If a student is worried about spelling a word correctly, he might choose a simpler alternative, limiting his expression.

✓ *Accurate communication*: With accurate spelling, punctuation and grammar our writing can be interpreted correctly – it communicates exactly what we mean to our audience. Just as a chemist mixes the correct ingredients together for an experiment, so we should include the right ingredients in our writing.

✓ *Technique matters*: In a sport, you need the correct technique to achieve a good performance; in writing, technique also plays a key role. The sports person practises for years to achieve an effortlessly good technique – the writer must get into good writing habits through years of training.

✓ *Hiding the technique*: With really good writing nothing intervenes between the reader and the text, the technique is completely hidden. A skilled story-writer immerses her audience totally in the fiction – the reader feels as though the normal world has disappeared, and only the story world exists. If there are technical errors, this distracts the reader from pure enjoyment.

✓ *Exam success*: A good grasp of the basics allows students to succeed in their exams. Even in those exams where accuracy of writing is not so crucial, an error-strewn piece will distract the examiner from the quality of what's been written.

✓ *Career success*: In the world of work, accurate writing is crucial. If an employer has lots of applicants to choose from, those whose application forms have spelling mistakes go to the bottom of the pile.

It's like watching a ballet: the dancers should look relaxed and at ease, leaving you free to enjoy the performance. The audience should be oblivious to the years of practice at the barre or the strained joints and bleeding toes.

Spelling

As you'll know, English is a tricky, irregular language. Although many words can be spelled by sounding out letters and phonemes, equally many cannot: the classic example is tough, bough, cough and dough. In order to spell properly, your students must:

✓ know the letter sounds and blends (phonemes)
✓ learn by sight those words that don't follow the phonic rules
✓ build strategies for handling tricky words
✓ be confident enough to 'give it a go', even when they make errors
✓ read and write a lot – practice makes perfect!

Why do spelling difficulties occur?

Problems with spelling occur for many different reasons. Identify the root cause of a student's difficulty, so you can find the most appropriate strategies to use. Difficulties might occur because of:

- Special educational needs – a student who has dyslexia, or who finds it hard to focus and behave.
- A lack of strategies – students who only use phonic approaches to decode or spell words, need to be taught strategies to cope with irregular words. Many students work these out for themselves, but some do not.
- A lack of reading experience – lots of reading inevitably helps with spelling.
- Lack of motivation – some students simply can't be bothered to check their work through for errors. They are not motivated enough to care.

Practical strategies for learning to spell

The best way to help your students learn to spell is to introduce them to a whole range of strategies – they can use the ones best suited to their own learning needs. I've divided up the suggestions here into different types of strategies – visual, aural, practical and so on. The more approaches your students have at their disposal, the better.

Visual strategies

Some strategies to teach students:

- ✓ *Look at the shape of words*: Examine the tall or short parts of words, or which bits come under or over the lines on a page. See a word as a unit – what kind of shape does it make?
- ✓ *Small in big*: Hunt out small words inside larger ones: 'out' and 'stand' in 'outstanding', 'move' in 'movement', 'extra' and 'ordinary' making up 'extraordinary'.
- ✓ *Prefix/suffix*: Use their knowledge of prefixes and suffixes to predict spellings – 'sub', 'dis', 'un', 'able', 'ful'. Work out the meaning of the prefix/suffix, to aid memory and comprehension. Visit the companion website for a link to a fun BBC prefix/suffix activity.
- ✓ *Highlighting*: Highlight the bit of a word that is likely to be tricky, using a highlighter pen. Focus on the tricky bit, so they are more likely to retain it.

✓ *Cut and colour*: When dividing a word up into syllables, write each syllable in a different colour.

✓ *Visual associations*: Link the word with a visual image or picture. Visualize the two 'oo's in 'look' as two eyes, see the 'e, y, e' in 'eye' as two eyes and a nose.

✓ *Visualization*: Practise 'seeing' words in their mind's eye. For instance, get them to close their eyes and visualize the word 'beautiful'. Now visualize it upside down and back to front. Visualize an incorrectly spelled word, with a huge red cross through it.

✓ *Does it look right?* After writing the word out, take a mental step back, see the word as a whole and ask the question 'Does it look right?' If not, try an alternative spelling.

And some visual strategies for the teacher:

✓ *Use visual aids*: Label resources and equipment in your classroom – seeing words all around is a great way to help vocabulary sink in. Offer lists of subject-specific words depending on the curriculum area where you teach.

✓ *Think big*: When creating labels and displays, go for large, clear fonts to make an impact. A word made up of one letter per A4 size sheet of paper has much more impact.

✓ *Introduce linked vocabulary*: When you're giving lists of words, for instance for spelling tests, utilize patterns and visual/aural links within the words. For instance, a list of words all using the suffix 'able', a list of words all using apostrophes for abbreviations (they're, we're, and so on), a list of words with the 'ue' sound at the end.

✓ *Use spelling tests*: The repetition of spelling tests, and their competitive nature, make them a good way to 'stick' words in your students' minds. Aim to differentiate the words you give whenever possible – you want them to be tricky, but not impossible, to learn.

Aural strategies

The following strategies are about hearing sounds and words in order to spell them. Encourage your students to:

✓ *Cut up words*: To help them spell longer words, practise splitting words into syllables. Make this more interesting by asking students to physically cut up words using scissors. Alternatively, the different syllables can be put on Post-its – one per sticky note.

✓ *Use rhyming word families*: Find groups of rhyming words and look for the patterns within these groups – advance, perchance and enhance.

A songwriter's rhyming dictionary makes a useful addition to your library.

✓ *Sound as spelled*: To remember irregularly spelled words sound them as they are spelled, not as they are said, emphasizing the 'wrong' bit in your head. For instance, 'sep – *ar* – ate', 'Feb – *ru* – ary'.

Physical strategies

A kinaesthetic approach to learning makes the learning stick better. It's also fun! Incorporate hands-on approaches whenever you can. These approaches are particularly useful for any students who have dyslexia. Ask your students to:

✓ *Sculpt the word*: Create artistic displays for really tricky words – make clay sculptures of key subject or topic words, to put on display.

✓ *Use invisible writing*: A correctly spelled word has a physical pattern – the hand must form the letters in a particular physical order. Write words with your fingers in the air, on your hands, on the desks, on a misted mirror, and so on. The physical act of writing the word over and over again helps create a physical memory.

✓ *Use physical memory devices*: To teach the word 'bed' make a 'bed' with index fingers and thumbs (left hand makes 'b', right hand makes 'd'). This helps students remember to put the 'b' and 'd' the correct way around.

Etymological strategies

Studying the roots of language gives your students access to the reason why words are spelled in a particular way. Encourage your students to:

✓ *Study the words*: Dig deeply into language to find good ways of learning and remembering spellings. Talk about how language changes and develops. When you're writing on the board, discuss the language you're using and where it comes from.

✓ *Figure it out*: Encourage your students to figure out where a word originates. Is it another language ('desperado') or maybe a visual description of an item ('T-shirt')? Visit this website www.krysstal. com/borrow.html for a useful list.

✓ *Study Greek and Latin roots*: Learn about Greek and Latin prefixes and suffixes – certain subjects (science, history) have lots of vocabulary from these ancient roots. The prefix 'hypo' in 'hypocritical' and 'hypodermic', or the letter combination 'psy' in 'psychiatrist' and 'psychology'.

For a fantastic resource for the study of where words come from, visit www.etymonline.com.

Call my Bluff
Have fun exploring unusual words, and their origins, by playing a game of *Call my Bluff*.

✓ Divide the class into groups of four or five students each.
✓ Give each group an unusual word, along with its proper definition.
✓ Each group must devise a set of definitions to give to the class.
✓ These should include the correct definition, with the other definitions made to sound as realistic as possible.
✓ The other groups must write down which person in each group they think gave the correct definition.
✓ When all the groups have given their definitions, read out the correct answers.
✓ The group with the most correct answers wins.
✓ To extend this game, get your students to find their own unusual words in a dictionary.

Independent learning strategies

Encourage your students to learn independently whenever possible, and to devise their own favourite strategies for learning spellings. They might:

✓ *Use mnemonics*: Memory devices and techniques are a great way to remember spellings, for instance remembering that stationery has an 'e' as in 'letter', or that you exaggerate the number of g's in 'exaggerate'. Encourage your students to devise their own memorable sayings or phrases. Find a link to a mnemonics list on the companion website.
✓ *Make use of spell-checkers*: The spell-checker on a computer is particularly helpful for those students who really struggle and whose writing is full of errors.
✓ *Find relationships*: Relate new vocabulary to words they already know, to give a memory hook ('obedient' and 'obey', 'prejudice' and 'prejudge'.) Use dictionaries to list all words that relate to each other.

Teaching strategies

There are also approaches that you can adopt within your teaching. Aim to:

✓ *Use imaginative resources*: Props are a great way to spark interest. In science you could challenge the students to learn spellings of some new equipment, then give anyone who can spell the term correctly the reward of using it first.

✓ *Have reference books available*: Equip your classroom with dictionaries, a thesaurus, a grammar reference book, a song writer's rhyming dictionary, a slang dictionary. Encourage students to use these reference books when they are writing.

✓ *Create a sense of 'ownership'*: Get your students to create their own lists of spellings to learn for a test, ones that they personally find particularly difficult.

✓ *It's not all about spelling*: Don't forget that good writing is not just about spelling properly. Set activities where your students write freely, without worrying about spelling.

✓ *Respect good mistakes*: There are two types of spelling mistake: those where the student has tried to apply prior knowledge, phonic awareness, or even knowledge about etymology, and those that are just a guess. When giving feedback, differentiate between the two.

✓ *Supply the vocabulary*: When you first approach a new topic area, in English or in another subject, supply your students with the words they will need. Have a short list of 'key words' for each lesson on the board before you start. Consider writing these up as your students watch, working through the spelling techniques needed with the class, rather than simply displaying them on an interactive whiteboard. Alternatively, supply the list on paper, for students to stick into their books. Find cross-curricular vocabulary lists at the companion website.

✓ *Encourage them to read – anything and everything!* One of the best ways to learn to spell is through repeated exposure to correctly spelled vocabulary. The quantity of reading that your students do inevitably has an impact on their success at spelling.

Look – Say and Think – Cover – Write – Check and Think

This is a popular technique for teaching spellings, and with good reason. Use it as a way to set words for your students to learn for a spelling test, or for students to practise vocabulary they find tricky to spell.

To get the most out of this approach, share the following strategies with your students:

- ✓ **LOOK** at the word – really look at it in detail. Focus on the overall shape as well as what it says and how it sounds.
- ✓ **SAY** the word out loud – can you sound it out using phonic techniques, or is it irregular? Split it up into its constituent parts/syllables. If it doesn't follow phonic patterns, sound it out anyway, focusing on the irregular bit (as in Feb – *ru* – ary). **THINK** about how you are going to remember it, focusing especially on the tricky bits. Can you devise some kind of memory aid to help you?
- ✓ **COVER** the word up and **WRITE** it.
- ✓ **CHECK** to see how you did. If you made a mistake, **THINK** about what the mistake was, why you made it, and how you could avoid making it again in future.

There are a variety of different ways to use this technique. You could:

- ✓ Put a specific list of words to learn in the 'look' column.
- ✓ Ask students to supply a list of words they would like to learn to spell properly.
- ✓ Stick a look – say – cover – write – check sheet in the back of exercise books. Get students to add any misspelled words into the 'look' column to practise.
- ✓ Use a coloured highlighter to identify tricky bits of the words.

A thought on homophones

Homophones (words that sound the same, but are spelled differently) often prove a particular challenge for students (and sometimes for their teachers as well). Find links between the meaning of the words and their spelling to make them easier to remember – the more unusual or wacky the idea is, the more memorable it will be. Here are a few examples:

✓ *Here and hear*: This homophone is easy, because the word 'hear' has an 'ear' in it. Emphasize the point by asking students to put their hand behind one ear and call out 'I h**ear** you!'
✓ *There and their*: The word 'their' has an 'i' in it; relate this to the fact that it means 'belonging to'. When you own something, you would say 'I own it'. This should help them remember the 'i' in the word.
✓ *Words with 'ere'*: Words with 'ere' in them tend to be words related to place, e.g. here, there, where. Remember this by using the phrase 'come over 'ere'.

Punctuation

The first priority when dealing with punctuation is to explain *why* it is so important to punctuate correctly. We need to punctuate our writing properly so that we can communicate accurately and effectively; so that the reader can focus on what we are saying, rather than how we are saying it; and so that we can succeed in our studies and get the best possible results in our exams and future careers. For more able writers, punctuation is also vital for finding a writing 'voice', and for expressing yourself in the tone that you want the audience to hear.

one of the best ways to explore the need for correct punctuation is to show your students a piece of writing with all the punctuation removed ask them to try and read the writing out loud the difficulties that they experience in doing this will help show the importance of punctuating properly in addition the weird experience of reading a paragraph that has no full stops commas speech marks or capital letters will help to empha size how important punctuation is as we have seen a strange or unusual approach will often stick in the minds of your children im willing to bet that this paragraph has grabbed your attention

Problems with punctuation

Punctuation errors occur for a variety of reasons; again it is well worth the teacher understanding the possible source of the students' difficulties.

– *Bad habits*: In those first couple of years of writing, when individual words become sentences, it's very easy for children to get into bad habits if they are not corrected repeatedly. Once these habits become ingrained, it is hard to reverse them.

- *Lack of understanding*: Some students don't understand how and when different types of punctuation mark should be used, or what purpose they serve. Emphasize the reasons why we punctuate to your class.
- *Lack of experience*: Once again, those students who are voracious readers simply meet more examples of punctuation than those who aren't. The student who has little experience of books and writing will lag behind.
- *Over-enthusiasm*: This is a common problem – students get carried away and write reams and reams but forget to punctuate it. The ideas rush into their heads, one after the other, and they are desperate to get them down on paper before they forget them. Over-enthusiastic writers often make excessive use of exclamation marks too!!!
- *The 'and' disease*: Some students use the word 'and' as an alternative to dividing their writing into sentences. Again, this may be about over-enthusiasm, or because they do not know how to use connectives and conjunctions.
- *Laziness*: Let's be honest: some students are not sufficiently motivated to check their work through for accuracy.

The pathway to punctuation

In reality, punctuation is not actually all that difficult – the range of punctuation marks is fairly limited, and the way that they are used follows a regular pattern. For your students to be able to punctuate properly, they need to take the following steps:

Learn the basic punctuation symbols and how/when to use them.

Understand why we punctuate:
it's used to add clarity and expression to writing.

When writing, form a full sentence in your mind
before you write it down.

Get into the *habit* of using punctuation every time you write.

Don't get into the *bad habit* of punctuating after you write.

Start to work with more advanced punctuation symbols.

Get your students to identify where they are on the pathway. See the companion website for a downloadable copy.

Practical strategies for learning to punctuate

The strategies below will help students who have got into bad habits with their punctuation.

Writing activities

✓ *Sentence in my head*: This approach reinforces the use of full stops.
  - Divide the class into groups. Ask each group to nominate a 'Punctuation Master'. This should be someone who is confident with punctuation.
  - Give each 'Punctuation Master' a sheet of small round black stickers, or a block of black Plasticine.
  - The challenge is for the students to form each sentence in their heads before they write it down.
  - Once they have a full sentence, they need to tell the 'Punctuation Master' what it is.
  - If he agrees that it is a full sentence, he allows them to write it down. He gives them a full stop sticker or a small bit of Plasticine to prove that he has checked the sentence.
  - Add an element of competition, e.g. the first group to all get five sentences, each with a punctuation mark.
  - Develop this activity by adding exclamation/question mark stickers.

✓ *'Cut and paste'*: Pick a suitable passage (for instance, from a story you've been studying), about a paragraph in length. Go through the text, Tippexing out all the punctuation. Make a note of each piece of punctuation you cut at the bottom of the page. The students must go through the text and add back in the missing punctuation. They should cross off the full stops, speech marks, commas, etc. at the bottom of the page, ensuring they use them all up.

✓ *Keep it simple*: For the student who experiences severe difficulties, use a simple target such as 'put a full stop at the end of every sentence'.

Reading/speaking and listening activities

✓ *Can I breathe now?* Choose a piece of text and remove all the punctuation. Display the text on your whiteboard, or give each student a copy. Read it together as a class, without taking a breath, because there are no full stops or commas. Afterwards, talk about how it felt to read a piece of writing with no punctuation.

✓ *Dramatic dialogue*: When you're reading stories as a whole class, ask for volunteers to play the characters. They must read out *only what their character actually says out loud*. The rest of the class judges whether they have done this accurately. This encourages students to look for speech marks while reading.

✓ *Read it back*: When students finish a piece of writing, ask them to read it out loud, either to you or to another student. As they read, they must only pause or use expression where they have actually punctuated. This pushes them to see the need for punctuation to convey meaning.

Interactive approaches

✓ *Traffic lights*: Display a piece of text on your whiteboard, with all the capital letters and full stops removed. You'll need a red pen (for stop – full stop) and a green pen (for go – capital letter). Work with the class to 'drive' through the piece of writing, adding back in all the full stops and capital letters. You can add in an amber light/orange pen for pauses, to show the use of commas.

✓ *Kung fu punctuation*: Both Ros Wilson and Phil Beadle have versions of this idea, which involves using physical movements and sounds linked to the different punctuation marks (punch and 'huh' for full stop, etc.). Use the link on the companion website to read a description by Phil Beadle of his approach. Why not develop your *own* version of kung fu punctuation, using the students' own ideas for the movements?

✓ *Speech mark sandwich*: I love this idea, which uses a simple metaphor to help students understand what speech marks do.
  – Explain to the students that you are going to make a 'speech mark sandwich'.
  – The speech marks are the bread, the speaking is the filling, and any punctuation is the ketchup or sauce.
  – Ask for volunteers to take on the role of bread, filling and sauce. (If you want to be really multisensory, use real sandwich ingredients to do this.)
  – Get the rest of the class to put together a 'speech mark sandwich'.

✓ *Action stations!* Here's another great idea for working on speech marks. Find a short film clip with plenty of speaking in it. Play the film clip to your class, with the sound turned down. The students must work in groups to write the dialogue (this could be comic as well as serious). Keep the clip playing in the background as your students write, so they can check their dialogue against the film. Get groups to read out their dialogue to the class with the clip playing.

Dealing with the runaway writer

You know those students who get so caught up in what they are writing that they forget to punctuate? The problem is, every time they do this, they get further into a bad habit for situations where they have to write quickly, such as in exams. It's far better to encourage them to use an alternative way of getting down their ideas – a brainstorm or a series of planning notes. Another useful method is to get them to record the writing first, then play it back to write it down, pausing the recording device after each sentence to give them time to punctuate.

Some thoughts on apostrophes

Approach work on apostrophes by explaining them logically: they replace a letter that is missing, or indicate ownership. Get your students to:

✓ *Find the missing letter*: Write out the words in full, for instance, 'it is' or 'they are'. Now cross out the 'missing letter' with a big red cross and replace it with an apostrophe to make 'it's' or 'they're'.

✓ *Apostrophe hit squad*: Challenge your students to spot (and photograph) examples of rogue or missing apostrophes outside school. You could set this as a homework task or simply reward any student who brings in an example.

✓ *Belonging*: This way of putting apostrophes in the correct place is one that I still remember from my own schooldays – I'm sure you do too! When trying to work out where to put an apostrophe, for example in the phrase 'the childrens books', turn the phrase around so that it says 'the books belonging to the children'. The apostrophe then goes at the end of 'children', before the 's'.

Grammar

When teaching grammar as a discrete subject, it's vital to keep the topic interesting and engaging, especially when trying to motivate reluctant writers. Direct teaching of grammar has the potential to be dry, likely to demotivate those we most want to encourage. In addition, some of the rules of English grammar are incredibly complex and difficult to understand. Even though I write for a living, there are still plenty of grammatical terms I have to look up first, before I'm able to teach them. Aim to introduce grammatical terminology as a natural part of working with language, rather than the study of grammar being about the 'naming of parts'. Remember: just because your students can spot a substantive clause, doesn't mean they know how to use it.

Problems with grammar

When we are babies learning a language as our 'mother tongue', we don't sit down and study the rules of grammar with our parents. Instead, the rules are internalized through the process of actually speaking a language – of using and hearing it on a daily basis. Students with English as a second language, or those who were brought up in a home where little Standard English was spoken, will often encounter difficulties with writing grammatically correct English.

As I pointed out at the start of this book, we write as we speak. If I find it hard to express myself fluently through speech, I'm going to find it tricky to express myself well in writing. This highlights the importance of speaking and listening work, focusing on the use of Standard English, both for English teachers and for those working at primary level.

Direct teaching of grammar

Some students see English as a 'soft' area of the curriculum, one that does not require expertise, just the ability to put pen to paper. Explain to your students that English has its own technique, just as science or maths does. In order to meet the technical demands, they must learn about the complex nature of language, thus freeing themselves to develop the imaginative aspects of their work.

Worksheet (or online) exercises that ask students to repeat a particular grammatical technique a number of times are useful. These reinforce learning that has taken place, but can be limited in terms of long-term understanding. One of the very best ways of learning about grammar is of course to pick apart pieces of text to see how they work.

I'm wary of an over-emphasis on teaching specific grammatical techniques to young writers, because what can happen is they pick up the message that they should chuck 'everything but the kitchen sink' into their writing. Remember: just because a piece of writing has lots of adverbs or adjectives or conjunctions in it, that doesn't necessarily make it a *good* piece of writing.

Practical strategies for developing grammar

Encourage your students to have fun with language: explore the effects created by different parts of English, and encourage them to experiment with working and reworking their writing to achieve different effects. Students find it hard to understand a topic via an abstract explanation: 'Today we will be studying comparative and superlative adjectives and adverbs, and the addition of the comparative and superlative suffixes "er" and "est".' But there's usually an active and practical alternative – see if you can find the activity I just described in the section below.

Writing activities

✓ *Sentence patterns*: Study patterns within sentences, and use these as a model for students to write their own.
   – *Show the class a sentence*: 'The boy crept slowly towards the haunted house, his body quivering with fear.'
   – Highlight the different parts of writing – noun, verb, adverb, etc.
   – Divide the sentence up into its constituent parts: 'The boy / crept slowly towards / the haunted house, / his body / quivering with fear.'
   – Now use this pattern to create their own sentences: 'The girl ran quickly towards the pile of presents, her face lighting up with joy.'
✓ *Stupid similes*: Invent a series of similes that don't work, either because they are wrong, or because they sound silly! Offer a prize for the worst example.
✓ *Magical metaphors*: This Pie Corbett activity is a lovely way of developing complex metaphors out of simple similes. It's great for showing how language can be moulded to create different effects.
   – Write a straightforward simile: 'The sun is like a yellow balloon.'
   – Take out the word 'like': 'The sun is a yellow balloon.'
   – Move the noun (or adjective/noun combination) to the front of the sentence: 'Yellow balloon sun.'
   – Finally, extend the idea by thinking about what the noun usually does. So, you might end up with: 'Yellow balloon sun, bobbing across the sky.'
✓ *Alphabetti spaghetti*: Use the format of the alphabet for lots of different word-based activities. Devise an alphabet of similes ('As angry as', 'As brave as') or an alphabet of adverbs ('angrily, brusquely, carefully'), perhaps combined with an alphabet of nouns 'the ant angrily ...').
✓ *Changing tenses*: Using a finished piece of writing, get students to change the tense throughout (or swap writing with a partner to do this). For instance, a story written in the present tense is changed to the past tense. What are the effects on viewpoint, tone and on the reader?

✓ *Avoiding adverbs*: Books on creative writing are full of warnings about adverbs being the sign of a 'lazy' writer: using an adverb to describe a verb lets the writer get away without being specific about the action or the person doing it, and consequently diminishes the picture that the reader creates in his mind. Contrast 'He walked slowly and fearfully up to the door' with 'He crept up to the door, terrified that the floorboards might creak and give him away'. Highlight adverbs in a piece of text, and come up with ways of rephrasing the text to replace them.

✓ *Prefix/suffix competition*: Give a prefix or suffix, for example 'un', 'ful' or 'able'. The students have three minutes to find the highest amount of words that can be made using it.

Reading activities

✓ *Simile sort out*: Play a 'simile sort out' game – give the students cards with different nouns, adverbs and adjectives on them. They must put these together to make interesting combinations.

✓ *Read and replicate*: Replicate the style of a published writer – you can either:
   – Ask each student to bring in a book. Call out a page number – the students turn to that page. Call out a line number – the students find that line. Now, they read the sentence on that line, and create a sentence of their own which mirrors the original.
   – Alternatively, the teacher has the book, and the students give the page and line number. The teacher reads out the sentence and the students create a similar one of their own.

✓ *Playing with adjectives*: Ask students to highlight all the adjectives in a piece of text. Discuss the effect that these adjectives have on the mood of the piece, for instance creating a scary atmosphere in a ghost-story. Now explore the effect that changing these adjectives would have:
   – Can they find better words?
   – What happens if all the adjectives are removed?
   – Is it possible to describe something *more* effectively without using adjectives?
   – What happens if they put in some 'boring' adjectives, such as 'nice' and 'OK' instead?

✓ *Effects of sentence length*: Find a passage that has a high level of tension (tension is often created by short sentences, which show a character's fear, or make the reader jumpy):

- Explore the length of each sentence, looking for a series of short sentences that heighten the tension.
- Which types of words are in these sentences?
- What is the shortest possible sentence, and what must it include?
- Can you break the rules to make a short sentence in fiction?
- What happens if these short sentences are joined together with conjunctives, or if subordinate clauses are added?

Speaking and listening/interactive activities

✓ *Rhythmic language*: Good writing has an inherent rhythm, which is created by a number of different aspects – the choice of vocabulary, the content of the writing, the length of sentences. Get your students to experiment with different ways of beating out the rhythms within sentences. For instance:
- the actual metre of the text, for instance a section of iambic pentameter
- the number of syllables in the words, without any particular emphasis
- in the way they would read the line, with a fast rhythm if it's action, or a slow one for descriptive texts.

✓ *Rhythmic writers*: Look at texts where the writers use rhythm in significantly different ways – for instance, contrast Ernest Hemingway with Toni Morrison.

✓ *Brainstorm 'strong' verbs*: A bank of really strong verbs is useful for creative writing – verbs that indicate a forceful or energetic action. Brainstorm to find a long list of these words to display on your wall:
- Give the class a sentence with a nondescript verb: 'He threw the football at his friend.'
- Brainstorm alternative verbs that might be used, and the effects these create.
- For instance, 'hurled', 'slammed' and 'thrust' all offer a stronger, more active replacement.
- To make this exercise active and hands-on, get two volunteers up to the front to demonstrate different ways of throwing a ball as you gather your verbs.

✓ *Super superlatives*: This activity sticks the idea of comparative and superlative adverbs/adjectives in your students' heads:
- Ask for three volunteers to come to the front.
- Give them an adjective (big, hard, small, tough, scary) without letting the rest of the class hear.

- They must make a series of frozen pictures to represent the three forms: big, bigger, biggest; hard, harder, hardest; and so on.
- The rest of the class guess the words.
- Now work together to put the three words into a single sentence: 'Although the dog was big, he had seen bigger dogs and he knew that the biggest dog of all was the English mastiff.'

Funeral for nice

This is a teaching idea that sticks firmly in the memory once you've heard it. A teacher who gave me the idea explained that her own teacher had done this with her when she was a child.

✓ Select a word you really don't want your students to use. In this instance it was (you've guessed it) 'nice'. Now hold a funeral for this word.
✓ Build a small cardboard coffin for the word. Add in some pieces of writing using this word or giving a eulogy to it.
✓ Challenge your students to write a burial service for the word.
✓ Take the class out into the school grounds. You will need a spade.
✓ Dig a hole and place the coffin inside.
✓ Take a pledge with your class that, from this day forwards, they will no longer use the word 'nice' in their writing.

The teacher who shared this story with me told me that, ever since that day, she has never been able to use the word 'nice' again!

Creative connectives and conjunctions

Get your students creating more complex pieces of writing, by joining their ideas together using connectives and conjunctions. Have a list of vocabulary available for your students to use. You can find a list to download on the companion website for this book.

You could display and use this vocabulary in a variety of ways:

✓ Hang them on a 'washing line' so students can pick out ones to use in their writing.

✓ Practise joining separate sentences together using a variety of connecting words.

✓ Give a set of words to use as a framework for a piece of writing: 'At first ... Next ... Later on ... Finally ...'

✓ Sort the words into boxes according to their different types – have these available for when students want to create a particular effect. You could have boxes with connectives for:
  - adding
  - sequencing
  - qualifying
  - cause and effect
  - illustrating
  - emphasizing
  - comparing.

 ✓ Visit the companion website for a link to a very useful PowerPoint slide show showing different types of connectives.

Some thoughts on paragraphing

Many students seem to have a 'blind spot' when it comes to paragraphing. The skill of paragraphing is essentially about learning to structure your writing: understanding the overall 'shape' of a piece of writing and the different ideas contained within it. Problems often occur where students start writing without having first mapped out what they're going to say. To help your students develop the skill of paragraphing:

✓ *Plan ahead*: Encourage them to see writing as something that needs an overall plan, *before* the task of working on the piece begins. They might:
  - Draw out a series of planning brainstorms, one for each paragraph (see Chapter 3 for more on this).
  - Write a few words to describe each event in a story, and sequence these using pegs and a washing line. Each event is extended into a paragraph.
  - Use the 'Paragraph in a box' idea described below.

✓ *Write paragraph by paragraph*: When you approach a whole-class piece of writing, insist they write one paragraph at a time. Set a sentence limit for each paragraph, and tell them to stop when they have completed this number (four or five is about right). Read the writing in groups, or as a class: discuss whether this would be an appropriate point for a new paragraph.

✓ *Non-fiction – point per paragraph*: In non-fiction writing, a single paragraph usually deals with a single point, giving a series of connected or related ideas. Ask your students to identify the point they are making in each paragraph of their writing, and where these points change from one set of ideas to the next. They should be able to boil the essence of a paragraph down to a single phrase – if they can't, it's probably not a single paragraph.

✓ *Use the 'four-step' technique*: This technique for essay-writing is explained in detail in Chapter 6 (p. 105). By using this approach, your students create a series of paragraphs, each giving a single point or idea and developing it.

✓ *Fiction – changes*: In fiction, a new paragraph generally comes with a change in the setting, the time, the characters involved, or the event being described. Get your students to write a four-paragraph story, to help them understand this:

– Paragraph 1 gives four or five sentences to describe a setting: 'The Planet Zog was a wild and desolate place …'

– Paragraph 2 makes a 'jump' in time: 'Many years ago the inhabitants of Planet Zog built a spaceship …'

– Paragraph 3 introduces some new characters: 'Zoglet had lived on Planet Zog all his life, but he had always longed to visit the stars …'

– Paragraph 4 describes an event: 'The spaceship's engine roared and the ship blasted off into space …'

Paragraph in a box

I love this idea which I was given by a fellow teacher. It's a very visual and concrete way of encouraging your students to write in paragraphs.

✓ Divide your class into groups. Each group makes a set of small boxes, using a net shape. Find a net shape on the companion website.

✓ These are their 'paragraph boxes'. Each box represents the contents of a single paragraph. Number the boxes.

✓ Now give the students a topic on which to write (or use a topic or text you're currently studying in class.)

> ✓ The students brainstorm all the ideas they'd like to include in their piece of writing. Each separate idea is written on a small slip of paper. The slips are sorted into piles, according to how the ideas relate to each other.
> ✓ The students label each box on the front with a word or phrase to say what the key idea is. They put the slips of paper relating to that idea inside the box.
> ✓ They decide what order they want the ideas to come in, and set out the boxes in this order.
> ✓ They then work together or individually to write the piece, taking each box in turn and creating one paragraph from the ideas held inside.

Handwriting

Handwriting is learned early, and any bad habits in forming letters or holding a pen tend to stay for the long term. To develop handwriting skills, and correct poor habits:

✓ *Use physical warm-ups*: Do a set of finger exercises at the start of a lesson to get your students engaged and to show them that writing is a physical, as well as an intellectual, activity. See p. 11 in Chapter 1 for ideas.

✓ *Use a pen-holder*: Offer a pen- or pencil-holder to those students who struggle to write correctly – a small rubber 'sleeve' slipped onto the pen or pencil which makes it easier to hold.

✓ *Consider the writing tools*: Using a ballpoint pen can cause difficulties, as you need to write firmly to form the letters. Consider the writing tools your students use, and whether they would find it easier to write with a felt-tip or a soft pencil, especially if they find good handwriting tricky. Challenge any departmental rules about the 'correct' writing tools.

✓ *Teach correct letter formation*: When children first learn to write, their teachers use demonstrations, activities and worksheets that teach the correct direction and order in which to form their letters. These worksheets are helpful for older students, who have picked up bad habits when forming their letters.

✓ *Use active approaches – whatever the age!* Use kinaesthetic approaches – drawing huge letters in the air, or taking the class outside to write enormous words in chalk on the playground floor.

✓ *Use ICT*: Give those students who find handwriting very difficult a break at times by allowing them to write on the computer. This lets them concentrate on the content of their work, rather than on its presentation.

✓ *Teach calligraphy*: Make handwriting fun and a source of pride. Teach calligraphy to your class to encourage students to take pride in their writing and to see handwriting as an art form.

✓ *Explore other forms of writing*: If you know a parent or member of staff who can write in Arabic or form Chinese characters, ask them to come and share their expertise with the class.

✓ *Keep an eye on their technique*: Watch for poor handwriting technique: don't assume all your students have learned the proper techniques early on, or maintained these over time. Students who are left-handed find handwriting particularly difficult, as they are covering the letters that they form as they write. Watch out for any difficulties they might experience.

✓ *Explore graphology*: Find some ideas for working on graphology below. These activities give a novel way of motivating your students to look at why clear handwriting matters.

Graphology

The graphology exercises below explore what our handwriting 'says' about us. Using graphology helps you motivate your students to analyse their own writing, and that of others. It also encourages them to consider the importance of presentation in writing and show them how our handwriting is as individual as we are. The subject itself is complex, and there's much scepticism over whether it is a 'science' or not. However, it offers the teacher a way of focusing on how handwriting looks and students find it very engaging.

For a set of notes to explain the technicalities of slope, flow, pressure, upper and lower case, etc. visit the companion website.

Whose handwriting?

Students love this exercise: particularly the challenge of working out whose writing they are analysing.

- ✓ Introduce your class to the art of graphology, using the notes on the companion website.
- ✓ Ask each student to write out a short piece of text on a loose piece of paper. Read this out loud to the class. When they have finished writing, ask them to draw a mark or symbol on the paper to help with identification later on.
- ✓ Collect in the pieces of paper, shuffle them, and hand them back out. Anyone who receives their own text, or a piece of writing they think they recognize, should hand it back to swap again.
- ✓ Give a set time in which to perform an analysis, using the graphology notes. Students can make notes on their analysis in their exercise books, but ask them not to write anything on the sample itself (so you can use it with another class if you want to). At the end of the time, they must try to guess whose sample they have been analysing.
- ✓ Bring everyone's ideas together by asking the students to stand up and give a brief analysis of the sample they have, and to name the person they believe wrote it. Did they guess correctly?

Analyse the adults

This is a highly motivational activity, which offers students the chance to 'analyse' their teachers. The preparation involved is definitely worthwhile, as you can reuse the exercise with different classes and age groups.

- ✓ Collect samples of handwriting from teachers and other staff at your school, asking them to write out a short piece of text (use the same text for each sample). Include some 'surprises', such as the head teacher, the caretaker and one of the catering staff. You can laminate them to protect them for reuse.
- ✓ Number the samples and make a separate note of whose writing corresponds to each number.

✓ In class, write a list on the board of the people whose hand-writing the class are going to 'analyse'.
✓ Hand out the samples: the students work in small groups on each piece of writing, swapping their sample with another group once they have finished.
✓ Compare the results, discussing your students' reasoning and finding out who has managed to identify the 'correct' writer.
✓ For added excitement, invite some of your sampled staff members in to hear more about how their handwriting reflects their personality.

Working with words

Finally, here are some interesting and engaging ways of working with words, many of which would make good starter activities:

✓ *Hunt the word*: This is a great way to familiarize students with using a dictionary. Introduce it as a 'game' or a 'contest', to increase motivation. It can be done by individual students, pairs, or in small groups, depending on the ability levels and on the number of dictionaries. Call out a word. The students race to find the word in the dictionary. As soon as they find the word, they raise their hand and identify the page reference. Extend this by reading out definitions, and identifying the type of word. Reward the winner by asking her to choose the next word to be hunted. You can use this game with vocabulary from different curriculum areas.

✓ *Invent the word*: Begin this activity by reading Lewis Carroll's 'Jabberwocky', which uses invented words, but ones that still make a kind of sense. Now ask your students to invent some words of their own. Perhaps they are aliens visiting the planet Earth, who have to invent words to describe the new things they see. Their words should have a tangible connection to the things they describe.

✓ *Invent the language*: In a similar vein to the idea above, this exercise works well in a speaking and listening or drama session. The students work in pairs, using the following scenario:

  – Student A is a visitor to a foreign country, and does not speak a word of the language.

- Student B is a local, who does not speak a word of English, only a foreign kind of goobledegook.
- Student A asks for directions in English.
- Student B answers in their invented language.
- After trying the scene, the students swap roles.
- Volunteers perform their scene to the class.

This exercise results in some hilarious improvizations, and also effectively demonstrates the different ways in which we try to communicate. After watching the performances discuss how we use body language and gesture to overcome difficulties in communication.

✓ *Word of the week*: Choose one word per week for your class to look at in detail. Get your students to make a huge poster of the word to go on the wall. Activities for the 'word of the week' might include:
  - the study of closely related words
  - exploration of the roots of the word
  - finding all rhyming words
  - analysing the category into which the word falls (verb, noun, etc.).

3

The Writer's Toolkit

Easy reading is damn hard writing.

Nathaniel Hawthorne

The writing techniques described in this chapter go together to make up the 'Writer's Toolkit'. The exercises and ideas given here will help you introduce and develop these techniques, and inspire your students to experiment with different ways of writing. Not every piece of writing will involve all of the techniques described here, but for extended or finished written work these steps are important in achieving the best possible result. Even the simplest piece of writing benefits from an understanding of audience, viewpoint, style, genre and so on. I've included some case studies in this chapter, to show you how the ideas given might work in practice.

Writing processes

The main processes involved in approaching a piece of writing, and a series of questions for your students (or for you) to ask, are listed below. For a copy of these processes, to download and share with your class, visit the companion website.

Preparing:

Find a starting point	*What can I use to inspire my writing?*
Select a form	*What's the best format to say this in?*
Know your audience	*Who is my writing aimed at?*
Think about your viewpoint	*Where do I stand in relation to my reader?*
Think about your style	*What kind of language should I use?*
Think about timing	*What tense and other time features do I use?*
Brainstorm your ideas	*What ideas do I already have?*
Research facts/information	*What else do I need to know?*
Map your ideas/points	*How are these ideas connected/sequenced?*

Select your material	*What do I need? What don't I need?*
Plan your writing	*How should I structure the piece?*

Writing:
DRAFT

Review	*What's good or bad about it and why?*
Edit	*How can I improve my piece of writing?*

REDRAFT

Check for errors (proofread)	*What technical mistakes have I made?*
Consider presentation	*What's the best way to present this?*

FINAL DRAFT

Review the finished product	*Is this as good as it could be?*
Evaluate the finished product	*How can I make it better next time?*

The three steps in bold/capitals do not have a question: this is because they are the points at which writing is actually taking place. Your students may be surprised at how much else there is to do when creating a piece of writing. Some of the steps are quick: a decision to be made. Others, such as redrafting, take much longer. The following sections provide more detail about these processes, with activities for you to use to examine and develop different techniques.

Finding a starting point

Starting points come from a whole host of different sources. The teacher's skill lies in finding a starting point that engages the class, and introducing it in a way that inspires the students to write. For instance, you might:

✓ *Dive straight into a fictional approach*: 'I found a handbag on my chair this morning when I came into my classroom. Shall I open it and see what's inside?'
✓ *Use the students' choice*: 'Here's a variety of resources you might like to use. Which ones will you choose to inspire your writing?'
✓ *Use the teacher's choice*: 'I want you to imagine the beach where this shell came from, and use that setting as a starting point for your story.'
✓ *Make a quick start*: 'Right, everyone, you've got one minute to brainstorm as many words as you can to use in your writing. The theme is "The weather". Three, two, one, go!'

✓ *Do an extended writing project*: Sometimes your original starting point will take you in lots of different directions, and end up creating opportunities for writing in lots of different forms.

The options for a starting point are as varied as you care to choose. You might use:

✓ an image
✓ a photograph
✓ facts and information
✓ ideas and thoughts
✓ a theme or topic
✓ vocabulary
✓ a piece of music
✓ a place (real or imagined)
✓ a film clip
✓ a piece of text
✓ a poem
✓ a prop
✓ a symbol
✓ a mystery that needs solving
✓ a challenge
✓ a viewpoint
✓ a question that needs answering
✓ responses to different sensory resources.

Case study: The supermarket car park

Starting point: The teacher shows the class a letter that has been received that morning at the school. The letter is from a local supermarket. They are asking whether they can buy a section of the school sports field, on which to build an extension to their car park. The money is badly needed to repair the leaking roof in the gym, and to build a new dance and drama studio. The head teacher has sent a copy of the letter to each class, so that she can get some responses from the students before she decides what to do. She would like them to draft a letter in response to the supermarket. (If you can get your head teacher to bring the letter into your classroom, and make the request in person, this adds a fantastic layer of realism to the story.)

From this inspirational starting point, the students could move on to:

✓ Write a letter in response to the supermarket.
✓ Hold a planning meeting with locals, councillors, representatives from the supermarket, and so on. Write the minutes of this meeting.
✓ Write a news report (for a newspaper, or scripted for the TV) on the controversy surrounding the supermarket's plans.
✓ Write a letter or email to the local newspaper from a variety of viewpoints – a concerned resident, a resident who wants more parking, a local cyclist protesting about the plans.
✓ Work as environmental consultants to write a report on the environmental impact of the proposed car park.
✓ Write a petition against the proposals; write a petition for the proposals.

 For a letter you can download to use with your class, see the companion website.

Selecting a form

In many instances, the selection of a form in which to write is a decision made by the teacher, because of the need to cover different types of writing. Aim to mix and match the form and the type of writing, so that you use a fictional form to write about a non-fiction theme, and vice versa. This adds a layer of interest for the students. It also allows you to experiment with different forms of writing in subjects such as History or Science.

You might get your students to write:

✓ a newspaper report about events in *Macbeth*
✓ a poem in response to a school trip to a nature reserve
✓ a recipe for 'My perfect book'
✓ a shopping list written by a Roman soldier, before he travels to England
✓ the script for a TV show in the style of *Question Time*, exploring the issues around climate change.

Using frames and frameworks

Frames and frameworks offer you a way to get your students working with different forms. The ideal approach for using a frame is to:

✓ share several examples of this particular form in use with the class
✓ encourage the students to identify the salient features of the form
✓ work through an example with the whole class, on the board, with the teacher modelling the correct way to use the form
✓ give those students who need it a frame to help them scaffold their writing
✓ encourage the students to write independently within a similar format.

Encourage your students to adapt the frame to suit their needs, rather than slavishly following the format they have been given. More able and older students could create frames for the rest of the class to use.

Visit the companion website for a link to a very useful booklet from the National Centre for Language and Literacy. This booklet includes a wide range of downloadable frames for writing.

Knowing your audience

Of course it's vital to know the audience for a piece of writing, because this determines the language we use, the style in which we write, the type of presentation we use, and so on. Your students should ask themselves:

✓ What will my audience expect to find in this kind of writing?
✓ Can I confound audience expectations in an interesting way?
✓ What type and level of vocabulary is appropriate for this audience?
✓ What style of writing is appropriate for this audience?

You can create some very interesting effects by encouraging your students to play around with writing for different audiences. Where the audience is a real one, this makes the writing task far more meaningful. There are a variety of real audiences you could use, as in these ideas.

✓ *Write for local schools and the local community*: There's a real audience right on the doorstep, made up of other people at your school and in the local area. Your students might:

- write a book aimed at young children in a local primary school, visiting the school to research the needs of their audience
- create a brochure or programme for a local event – a flower show, a festival, a theatre group
- write some anti-litter posters to display in a local park
- create books for your school library, or for other teachers to use with their classes.

✓ *Write for the internet*: Go online to publish your students' writing: seeing their work online is an excellent way of motivating your students.

✓ *Write to an author*: Get your class to write to an author they admire. Many authors happily respond to the letters or emails they receive from their readers. Look into arranging an author visit to your school.

Case study: School magazine

I have very fond memories of having my work published in a school magazine when I was a child. This was one of the factors that led me to become an author myself. For the past few years I've been working with a local school to create an official school magazine, which is published three times a year. Our audience is a truly 'real' one of other students, parents, grandparents, teachers and local people.

The students love seeing their work in print, being read by their peers and their families. They get to write in a variety of forms, learning about each one as we create the magazine. They're also involved in taking photos, and in designing front covers. I run a 'guest editor' slot, which allows one student to edit the magazine, deciding on the theme and on the order of the content.

In our magazine, we've included:

✓ word searches
✓ interviews (with staff and parents too – last issue we interviewed an aerospace engineer)
✓ competitions
✓ quizzes
✓ reports on school trips
✓ poetry and stories
✓ our favourite ... pets, books, hobbies, toys, etc.
✓ how to ... build a hot air balloon, make a paper aeroplane, etc.
✓ recipes, and much much more.

Thinking about viewpoint, style and timing

With an understanding of form and audience, your students can consider viewpoint, style and timing. Getting these three elements right, and learning how to experiment and approach them in creative ways, is a key factor in quality writing.

Viewpoint

Viewpoint describes where the writer stands in relation to the reader – usually either first person ('I did this ...') or third person ('He did that ...'). Encourage your students to experiment with different viewpoints, exploring how a piece of writing works with a first- or third-person narrative. By looking at different viewpoints you encourage the skill of empathy, particularly when writing a first-person narrative.

To get your students experimenting with a first-person viewpoint:

✓ *The toy's story*: Ask them to bring in a favourite toy, and bring in an old one of your own. Start the lesson by showing them your toy, and telling them its story (using a 'toy-like' voice if you're brave enough). The students could then:
  – write the story about the day that the toy came to school, from the perspective of the toy, using a first-person narrative
  – take the toy on a trip around the school, viewing it through their eyes, thinking what its thoughts and feelings would be and writing about them
  – write the story of an adventure that the toy had, in the style of the film *Toy Story*.
✓ *Diary writing*: Write the diary of a famous person or historical character, aiming to capture their 'voice'. This works well in English (the diary of a character in a set text) and also in other curriculum areas, such as History, RE and Science.
✓ *The object's view*: A more unusual approach is to use a character that is actually an object: for example, the viewpoint of the football that was used during the FA Cup Final. How did the football feel about all those fans chanting? How did it feel about being kicked so hard, and ending up in the back of the net?

It's particularly useful to get your students writing from a viewpoint and with a view that is not their own, especially when studying controversial topics. Get them to state what their view on the topic is on a postcard, then swap with a partner who has the opposing view. They must write a piece from a perspective that is diametrically opposed to their own.

Style

Many aspects go together to make up the style of a piece of writing. The writer's decision about the appropriate style to use depends a great deal on the form and audience. The most successful writers have a style all of their own – the elements combine to create a writing voice that is at once instantly recognizable and uniquely their own.

To get your students thinking about style:

✓ Ask them to study several extracts of writing – include extracts from:
  – a children's storybook
  – a literary novel
  – a newspaper report
  – a history textbook
  – a recipe.
✓ Examine the style that the writer uses in these extracts, using the checklist given at the companion site (see below).
✓ Discuss the effect of these different aspects of style.
✓ Rewrite one of the pieces, in a completely different style, choosing a totally different audience.
✓ For instance, a dry piece of writing from a history textbook is rewritten in the style of a football match report; a tabloid news report is rewritten in the style of a children's story.

 Find a copy of a 'Studying style' checklist at the companion website.

Timing

One of the most important features of timing is the ability to write in (and stick to) the correct tense, something that many students find difficult. As well as considering which tense to use, encourage your students to play with other aspects of timing, particularly when writing creatively (for instance, jumps in time, use of slow-motion effects, flashbacks, and so on).

It is helpful to talk about the logic of tenses. Encourage your students to consider where they stand in relation to the piece of writing. Are they describing something that happened in the past, that is happening in the present, or that will happen in the future? Here are some thoughts to share:

✓ *The story*: The majority of stories are written in the past tense. When we invent a story it is created first in our heads, then retold on paper. Encourage students to run a 'film' of the story in their imagination, 'watching' the characters and the events that take place. Then, writing the story becomes a case of describing the events that have just taken place, using the past tense.

✓ *The essay*: When writing an essay (except if describing historical events) we give an interpretation of a text or situation, making a series of statements that we believe to be true. These interpretations or statements are made at the moment we write the essay. Consequently, it's logical to use the present tense.

✓ *Instructions*: When writing a list of instructions to build a piece of furniture, we are describing the series of actions that somebody would need to take in their 'present'. Consequently, we use the present tense, with a series of commands, for instance 'First, nail the wooden board into the base …' If the instructions are for something that will happen in the future (for instance details of a forthcoming school trip), the future continuous tense will be appropriate, for instance 'Next week we will be going to …'

✓ *Recounts*: A recount inevitably uses the past tense, because it describes something that happened in the past. Typically a recount uses connectives to signal time – 'Last week we went to … First we … Then we …'

Encourage your students to think carefully about the timing and pace of their writing. This is particularly helpful when writing fiction. There are various ways in which timing/pace are created:

✓ *The balance of description and action*: Much depends on the balance of these two features. If a story is heavily descriptive, this slows the pace right down; a story that is pure action, without so much as an adjective, is fast-paced and gripping. Get your students to write a close, descriptive study, and then a fast, pure action story. How do they differ?

✓ *Slow-motion moments*: Many films make use of slow motion at a pivotal point in the story. Encourage your students to consider which moments in their writing might deserve the 'slo-mo' close-up treatment and why.

✓ *Sentence length*: The length of the sentences in a piece of writing has a surprisingly strong impact on its pace. Long sentences slow down the pace of the writing, while short sentences add pace and movement and often a tense, edgy sensation.

✓ *Punctuation*: Punctuation also has a strong influence on the pace of writing: a sentence with lots of commas slows the reader down, a piece using short sentences and full stops has a punchy, jerky feel.

The two examples below demonstrate how descriptive writing can give a slow pace, whilst a more action-packed style will give a piece that reads in a much faster way. You can find a copy of these passages on the companion website, to download and discuss with your class.

Example 1: Descriptive (slow pace)
Jane stood in front of the doorway, collecting her thoughts, delaying her decision until the last possible moment. As she waited for her courage to arrive, like a slow-train moving into the last station on the line, she studied the door in front of her. It was crafted from an ancient-looking wood, the handle a simple metal ring. Jane glanced down as she stretched her arm out towards the handle. Her hand was shaking, and the deep red nail polish on her nails reminded her of blood. She retracted her hand and took two deep breaths, brushing her fringe from her face with her pale fingers. She stood a while, contemplating everything that might happen once she went inside. Then, at last, she was ready. She summoned up every ounce of courage in her body and grabbed the handle. Turning it slowly, and pushing the heavy door open in front of her, she stepped into the hallway.

Example 2: Action (fast pace)
Jane ran to the door. She grasped the handle and turned it. Pushing the door open she moved inside. She sped down the hallway and reached the room at the far end. No one there. She turned and ran in the opposite direction. No sound of him. No sign of him. Where on earth could he be?

Sequencing

Your students also need to think about the best sequence for the material they wish to use. Typically, writing is best presented in a chronological format, or by moving from the general to the specific, for instance in a discussion text or essay. However, this rule can be broken. To work out the best sequence of ideas to use, your students could:

✓ experiment with presenting the ideas and sequence in a visual way (this works well for stories – see the case study below)
✓ physically move ideas around, for instance by writing ideas on cards and pegging these to a line
✓ use a storyboard to map out their ideas in pictures, before writing them down
✓ use a timeline to show what happens when.

When writing fiction, students can get some great effects by playing around with the sequence of events in their plot. The two key ways of doing this are:

✓ *Foreshadowing*: The writer 'foreshadows' events that will happen later on, by making subtle references to key themes within the story. For example, a shiver runs down the spine of a character as she passes a locked room, or the sun moves behind a cloud when the villain appears.
✓ *Flashbacks*: The writer 'jumps back' to events that happened earlier in time. An interesting effect can be created by starting almost at the end of a story, and then jumping back to the beginning.

Case study: The Story Making© Project

This project has been running at my children's primary school for the last few years. It could very easily be adapted to be used with secondary students. The idea is the brainchild of the International Learning and Research Centre – see the companion website for links. The children learn about the sequencing and patterns of narratives through imitation, innovation and invention.

✓ The children take a well-known story – for instance, *The Three Little Pigs* or *The Very Hungry Caterpillar*.
✓ They break down this story into the key points during the plot.
✓ These key points are represented in a visual way, linked by arrows.

> ✓ The children tell the story orally, using movements alongside the speaking, to help them remember and retell the story in a vivid way.
> ✓ Afterwards, the children take the pattern of the traditional story and adapt it, writing their own versions. For instance, *The Very Hungry Tiger*.
>
> The children have presented their stories to a range of audiences – to an invited audience of parents and carers, and also to children at our local preschool.

Brainstorming

The brainstorm (sometimes also referred to as the spidergram or scattergram) has become ubiquitous in our classrooms, and with very good reason. It has a whole range of uses within the classroom, including:

✓ as an excellent way of gathering ideas together
✓ for a whole-class session when first introducing a new topic
✓ imposing an initial structure on our thoughts and ideas
✓ helping to develop lateral thinking, for instance by using arrows to create a series of sections and subsections.

Students use brainstorming in many different areas of the curriculum, not just in their English or literacy lessons. Because they are so commonly used, it's worth thinking up some new approaches so that we keep our use of the technique effective, fresh and interesting. Here are some ideas:

✓ *Use colours*: Colours help segregate ideas into different areas or types, and make a brainstorm more visually appealing. When creating a brainstorm on 'Our world' as a geography topic, use blue for water-related ideas, green for ideas connected to plants, brown for the land, and so on.
✓ *Make it big!* Big (or preferably huge) forms of writing are particularly appealing. Take your class into the hall, or another open space, to create an enormous brainstorm on your topic. Do it directly on the tarmac outside, with outdoor chalks, or on a long roll of paper.

✓ *Make the brainstorm active*: Get your students moving around, sharing and swapping ideas, so that the learning becomes active and interconnected.

  – Divide your class into groups and give each group a different keyword to write in the centre of a large sheet of paper. This is their starting point for thinking about a theme or text.

  – For instance, if the text was Arthur Miller's *The Crucible*, the keywords could be fear, witchcraft, religion and paranoia.

  – Give the groups five minutes to write all their ideas around their keyword on sticky notes, and stick these onto their brainstorm.

  – Now ask the students to 'take a wander' around the room, looking for any sticky notes that relate somehow to their own part of the theme.

  – Trade/swap/copy ideas between the groups, looking for how these themes link one to another.

✓ *Use a tight focus*: Brainstorms can also be used with a tighter focus, for instance brainstorming all the vocabulary connected to a single word (such as 'cat') in order to write some poetry.

Note: in recent years the notion came about that the word 'brainstorm' might be offensive to people who have epilepsy. When some research was done by the National Society for Epilepsy, it was found that the majority had no problem at all with the term. In fact, it was suggested that it might be offensive to those with epilepsy to suggest that they were so easily offended.

As the PC debate about language rages, suggested alternatives for brainstorm include the amusing sounding:

  – cloud burst
  – mind shower
  – thought festival
  – and brain dump!

You might like to offer your students a prize for the most amusing alternative they can devise.

Researching

Once they have gathered the ideas they have, and established what they already know, your students need to decide what other information or facts are needed for their writing. This might mean reading some texts to explore their use of language, before writing a similar text of their own. It could be a matter of identifying quotes to use in an essay on a set text. It might be a complex task such as researching an entirely new topic in depth. These days, there are a host of potential sources for research:

✓ *Texts*: I use the word 'texts' rather than 'books', because some of the most helpful information may be found in magazines and news-papers. Before doing research, equip your students to do it effectively, for instance teaching them about contents pages and indexes. So long as it's appropriate (i.e. on a *copy* of any school or library books), I like to see research texts covered in highlighter pen, with scribbled notes in the margins, and so on.

✓ *People*: Interviewing an 'expert' can offer valuable research material. Your 'experts' might be from local businesses, from families, etc. Alternatively, your students could write to authorities on the topic.

✓ *Trips*: For many students, a class trip is one of the most exciting events of the school year. A trip also offers a chance to take a fresh perspective on a topic or to gain first-hand information.

✓ *ICT*: Teachers can now draw on a range of ICT resources; however, it is surprisingly hard to use these effectively without consuming vast amounts of time. There is just so much material out there, that it is easy to find yourself moving laterally from the original point of your research (although this is not necessarily always a bad thing).

 The internet, for all its upsides, does have plenty of potential downsides. There is the danger of plagiarism – see the companion website for a useful link to help you identify and prevent it. There are also concerns about the reliability of the information you find – see the case study below for an interesting way to make this point.

Focused research

Help your students learn how to research efficiently, by:

✓ *Identifying the information that is needed*: Get your students to create a list of questions they need or want answered. Their research should focus on answering these questions, with the aim of answering a set number of questions in a single lesson.

✓ *Providing focused research material*: If you are researching in a school library or learning resource centre, liaise with the librarian before the lesson to find the texts that will be most useful to the students.

Present these on a 'research table' for the class to explore. For internet research do some study ahead of time, and give your students a list of the best or most useful websites.

✓ *Keeping them 'on task'*: Use targets and reviews to achieve this – after 15 minutes you stop the class and ask one or two students to talk about what they have discovered. Alternatively, give each student a worksheet to complete, identifying what was discovered during the lesson, and where it was found.

✓ *Setting research as a homework task*: The beauty of this approach, particularly with a large project, is that your students naturally differentiate their learning. The more able or enthusiastic ones seize the opportunity to delve deeply into a subject. Provide the less able or less well-motivated with a well-targeted set of homework questions.

Case study: Bill Gates is dead

This activity was suggested to me by an ICT teacher, to demonstrate to students how unreliable the internet can be. It helps them understand they should not take the first thing they read on the internet as the 'truth'.

✓ The teacher explains to the class that he has just heard some bad news: Bill Gates, the founder of Microsoft, is dead.
✓ The students are asked to find out what happened. They start by Googling the phrase: 'Bill Gates is dead.'
✓ They are rewarded with over 2 million hits!
✓ The top site to appear is the website: www.billgatesisdead.com!
✓ The students spend the lesson finding out how he died, etc.

The lesson finishes with the teacher telling the class that Bill Gates is alive and well. As an extension, discuss with your students which sites they can trust and which ones they should be wary about.

Mind-mapping

The mind-map is the brainstorm's 'big brother': if you haven't used this technique yet, do give it a try. It is sometimes also referred to as the 'concept map'. While the brainstorm gives us an effective way of noting initial ideas or information, the mind-map offers a wonderful method of organizing these points before we start to write. Mind-maps are useful for a whole range of reasons:

✓ They give a structured overview of data or information that you already have, or can be used to brainstorm initial thoughts on a particular topic.

✓ They help give structure to complex ideas, those that are too difficult or diverse to keep in your head at one time.

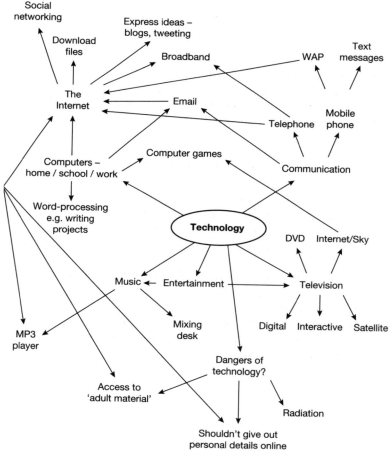

Figure 3.1 Mind-map: *'What role does technology play in your life?'*

✓ They allow you to include information that has a lateral connection to the main topic, exploring different tangents and connections that might not be apparent at first glance.

✓ They work in much the same way that our brains work: we store huge amounts of information in our brains by making connections between different facts, ideas and so on.

✓ They can be used across the range of curriculum subjects, and for a huge variety of different topics.

As with brainstorms, colours are very useful for making a mind-map more effective, especially if these colours are linked to the topic and sub-topics being studied. Perhaps the best way to understand the mind map is to look at an example. The mind-map pictured in Figure 3.1 is based on the question: 'What role does technology play in your life?'

Selecting material

Deciding what to include, and what to leave out, is often a real challenge, especially under exam conditions. Students are so keen to include everything they know that they fail to answer the question and run out of time. Selecting suitable material is a vital skill to learn. It depends a great deal on the purpose of the writing: is it to answer a specific exam question, to study a topic in detail, to entertain, to inform?

Here are some thoughts about teaching the selection of material to your students:

✓ *Identify the purpose of the writing*: Take time to discuss this: why are they writing on this particular topic, and what will their audience expect? Use questions to guide your discussion:
- Is the writing a brief summary, or an in-depth study?
- Are you trying to entertain or inform the audience?
- What does the reader most need or want to know?
- Is the purpose to answer the question in a way that gains maximum marks?
- If so, what needs to be included?

✓ *Answer the question*: To succeed in their exams, your students need to answer exam questions as accurately and concisely as possible, including just the right amount of information and material to gain maximum marks. There are lots of tips about how to do this in Chapter 6 (Essay writing) and Chapter 13 (Writing and assessment).

✓ *Make it interesting*: A successful piece of writing, whether fiction or non-fiction, must gain the interest of its reader. For example, in a piece of fictional writing, where there is no 'right' or 'wrong' answer, your students must learn to grip the reader, find interesting vocabulary and invent exciting events. You can find lots of ideas about effective creative writing in Chapter 7.

✓ *Something unusual*: Given 30 pieces of writing on the same topic, it is the one with a touch of originality that will stick in the reader's or examiner's mind. This could be the writer who expresses herself with a dash of style, who includes an unusual but telling fact or detail, or who demonstrates the ability to think laterally around a subject.

Case study: Cut it out!

This activity is great for helping your students think about how and why to select or cut vocabulary from a piece of writing. The initial stream of consciousness activity also makes a great warm-up for a writing lesson.

✓ Your students will be writing for a short time – about two or three minutes is enough.
✓ When you say 'go' they start writing; they must keep going until you say 'stop'. Their pens must not leave the paper.
✓ If they get stuck, they should keep writing the same word over and over again until they get unstuck.
✓ They should not worry about punctuation or spelling.
✓ You can set a specific topic on which to write, or they can just write down any words or thoughts that come into their heads.

This original stream of consciousness is then extended into an exercise focused on editing and selection.

✓ Count the number of words on the page and write the number at the bottom.
✓ Now, cut this number exactly in half, by crossing out any words that seem irrelevant or unimportant. The writing does not need to make sense – the choice of what to cut is up to them.
✓ When this is done, they must cut the number in half again, so that they end up with exactly a quarter of the original word-count.

✓ The remaining words are written out, one per slip of paper. These are arranged to create a word picture or poem. Why did they save or select these particular words?

Planning

Many students find it hard to understand why they should plan their writing, rather than plunging straight into it. In lessons, we can help them plan their work with a whole-class introduction to the lesson, during which we identify what should be included in their writing. In exams, though, students often seem fearful of 'giving up' the amount of time that a plan would take them to write. However, a good plan is absolutely crucial to an effective piece of writing, and will save time in the long run. A well-thought-out plan has many benefits, particularly in an exam:

✓ It gives a clear structure to a piece of writing.
✓ It helps the student stay on track when answering a question.
✓ It ensures that everything of relevance is included.
✓ It helps stave off panic if the student's mind suddenly goes blank halfway through an answer.
✓ If there isn't time to finish the answer, it allows the examiner to see the points that would have been included.

When planning for an extended piece of writing, I find it useful to ask students to create a series of brainstorms, one for each paragraph or part of the work. This method is useful because:

✓ It encourages your students to structure and paragraph their writing correctly;
✓ It is a time-efficient method of planning;
✓ It allows the overall planning of the writing as a whole;
✓ The student can go back and add in additional ideas, quotations, facts to include, and so on.

From first draft to final draft

The pressure to cover the curriculum can lead to a situation where we get our students to 'bang out' pieces of writing one after the other, with only

59

minimal thought given to drafting, reviewing, editing and redrafting the work. When time is short, the temptation is to have at least one quantifiable piece of writing to 'prove' that we have dealt with each subject area. We have surely all experienced the student who brings us a piece of rough writing, and claims to have 'finished' the work. However, many of the skills of effective writing are learned from the processes that take place between the first and final drafts.

 Visit the companion website to find a list of the skills involved in developing a draft into a final piece of writing, to download and share with your students. To help your students practise drafting, reviewing, editing and redrafting:

- ✓ *Quick draft*: Encourage students to see their first attempt at writing a piece as a 'quick draft', setting a short length of time to keep them focused.
- ✓ *Test draft*: Use practice answers written under timed test conditions as a handy first draft (for instance for a piece of coursework). Keep rough drafts by GCSE-level students – you never know when they might come in handy.
- ✓ *Draft on the computer*: Encourage your students to draft using a word processing program, both at home and in class.
- ✓ *Read it back*: When a student brings you a 'finished' piece of work, ask them to read it back, either to you or to a partner. This helps them learn about redrafting to correct errors and to make writing sound better.
- ✓ *You be teacher*: Get students to swap first drafts over and 'be teacher', marking, commenting on and correcting their partner's work.
- ✓ *Set a focus*: For weaker writers, it can be disheartening to redraft their work, because there are so many mistakes to correct. For these students, set a specific focus for the redraft. This could be to check spellings, make sure full stops are in place or divide it up into paragraphs.

Case study: Two stars and a wish

This primary school approach translates very well into the secondary classroom. It can be used to assess writing, and also other types of learning. It's especially useful for peer assessment, because sometimes students can be rather harsh on their peers. It encourages them to come up with some positives alongside the negatives.

The student is given 'two stars and a wish' to assess the work: the 'two stars' are two things that are good about the writing, the 'wish' is something that could be improved upon, next time around.

Presenting the final draft

Encourage your students to be creative about presenting finished pieces of writing. Here are some suggestions:

✓ *Use imaginative presentation techniques*: With many pieces, the form of final presentation can be both imaginative and attractive. For an 'ancient' historical document, use the old favourite of staining the paper with tea or coffee, and then burning or tearing the edges slightly. For a children's book, get the students to create the book cover using a software publishing program.

✓ *Let your students have a say*: Your students will have their own ideas about presentation, often more imaginative or interesting ones than the teacher. Let the students have an input into the final presentation, to give them a sense of ownership of the work.

✓ *'Publish' the work*: Having a real audience is incredibly motivational. You could publish your class's final drafts, either as a class book of writing or perhaps via the internet.

✓ *Pass it around*: Get other staff at your school involved in reading and commenting on your students' writing. When a student does a particularly good piece of work, send her to show it to the head teacher or the reception desk staff. Ask her if she will read from it in an assembly, or allow you to feature it in a display.

Reviewing and evaluating

Finally, your students' writing benefits from time spent on reviewing and evaluating. This might take place as a whole-class activity, in which the students share their work and look at each other's writing. It could be an individual activity, in which students complete a worksheet asking them questions about the finished work. Asking our young writers to take this step, rather than viewing it as a part of marking, saves time for the teacher. More importantly, it encourages our students to look back at a completed piece of writing and consider the content, structure, use of language, punctuation and so on. By analysing their own work in this way, we can help them learn to set targets for the development of their writing.

The review and evaluation could focus on one particular area, for instance how technically accurate the work is, or how interesting and relevant they have made the content. Alternatively, you might ask your students to look at the steps listed at the start of this chapter, and consider which areas they still need to develop, and where they have been successful.

4

The Motivated Writer

Pleasure in the job puts perfection in the work.

Aristotle

In every school, no matter how 'good' it is, there will be some students who are simply not motivated to write, or who find writing a huge challenge. You know the ones I mean: every word is a struggle, like getting blood from a stone, to use the familiar cliché. This chapter deals with different ways you can motivate and inspire your students to write, and looks at how you can encourage them to keep on writing once they have started.

Getting them writing

How, then, do we get our students to write? Here are some initial ideas and tips for motivating your students, which will work with most age groups, and in all areas of the curriculum. Many of these ideas are explored in greater detail further on in this chapter.

✓ *Give them a reason to write*: When we ask our students to write, our motivation as teachers might be to cover the curriculum, or to help our students pass their exams. Don't forget, though, that your students also need some kind of motivation for their writing. Find ways to make the writing 'real', ways to inspire your students, ways to make them want to write.

✓ *Create an atmosphere for writing*: Create an atmosphere in which writing feels easy and natural. This could be as simple as having a quiet and positive working environment, achieved through good classroom management techniques. It might also mean creating a 'mood' in your classroom that inspires your students to respond through the medium of writing.

✓ *Get the 'correct' behaviour for writing*: Unless your students behave, the atmosphere in the classroom will not be conducive to good writing, or indeed to any writing at all. To get your students writing properly, you will need to help them develop skills such as focus, concentration and self-discipline.

✓ *Make the writing seem like fun*: Make a game of some writing tasks, for instance using the format of a popular TV programme. Use a stop-watch and prepare your class to start with the command: 'Ready, steady, write!'

✓ *Use 'warm-up' exercises*: When an athlete is preparing to run, or a dancer to dance, they warm up their bodies before they begin. In the same way, use 'warm-up' writing exercises to prepare your students to write.

✓ *Keep it topical*: Ask your students to write about something that they find genuinely interesting to help motivate them. Utilize the latest craze as a basis for their writing – TV programmes such as *I'm a Celebrity, Get me out of Here* or the latest fads in toys or computer games. When choosing a text for your students, make sure it's up to date and engaging. The internet also is a wonderful and topical resource for inspiring writing.

✓ *Work to their strengths*: Let your students write in the form or style that suits them when you can. A good way of doing this is to use a group 'project' where different students work on different aspects of the task.

✓ *Challenge them*: In my experience, students are motivated by work that they see as really challenging – work that you might feel is above their current level of ability. Some students view English as a light-weight subject, in contrast to the more technical demands of Science or Maths. Defy this assumption: teach them about extended metaphors, iambic pentameter, pathetic fallacy, whatever their age!

✓ *Remove the stress*: Some of your weaker students might be fearful about writing, rather than lacking in motivation. Perhaps they associate a sense of failure with the act of writing, especially if they have a specific difficulty with technique. If this is the case, on occasions tell them to write without worrying about the technical aspects of their work, such as spelling and punctuation. This will free them up to enjoy their writing.

✓ *Remove the blocks*: Similarly, some students are blocked in their writing, perhaps because of a fear of failure or of getting it wrong. The 'stream of consciousness' technique (see p. 58 in the previous chapter) offers a great way to free up their writing. Have a 'free writing' table where students can go to scribble, to make notes, to experiment.

✓ *Offer a reward*: We all work best when there is a carrot ahead of us, rather than a stick behind. Work out what will best motivate your students in their writing, whether this is stickers, merits or Mars bars. Have high expectations of what your students can achieve, and reward them when their work really deserves it.

✓ *Show that writing is relevant*: Talk to your students about the role of writing in their own lives: text messages, emails, the internet, magazines. Use these contemporary forms of writing as a resource to inspire your students.

✓ *Show that writing is important*: Talk to your classes about why writing is important, offering your own ideas and asking your students about their feelings. Talk with them about how we write for a whole range of reasons: to communicate, for pleasure and self-expression, to remember things, to pass exams, to be successful in a career.

✓ *Show yourself as a writer*: Let your students see you writing as much as possible: on a blackboard or whiteboard, on your interactive screen, on their work. Articulate the writing process to show your class the intellectual steps that writers take as they work. For more on the teacher as writer, see the companion website.

✓ *Offer yourself as an inspiration*: It is the teachers who were most passionate about their subjects and their teaching whom I remember from my schooldays, the ones with that indefinable 'spark'. Sometimes we get bogged down in the minutiae of the daily grind, on the curriculum, on success criteria, on Ofsted, on paperwork. Never forget that you have the ability to truly inspire your students! Show them how much you love writing, and how excited you are about the work that they produce.

Make it clear to your students that writing is as much about process as product. Sometimes, get them to throw away their writing after they've experimented with a piece – perhaps even turn it into a paper aeroplane and chuck it out the window if you're brave!

Keeping them writing

Once motivated, students often start to write with enthusiasm, but then run out of steam halfway through the more extended pieces of work. Here are some tips for keeping that motivation to write going once you have got them underway.

✓ *Set 'amount' targets*: Ask the class to write a specific amount, depending on their age and ability level, and on the type of task set. Your target might range from five words or one line of writing, to half a page or 50 words. For your weakest writers, put a mark on the page and ask them to write down to this point.

✓ *Set 'time' targets*: When you set a writing activity, always be specific about the length of time in which it must be done. Generally speaking, the shorter the time, the more focused the writing will be. Split up your lessons by setting short, timed writing tasks alongside a variety of non-writing activities.

✓ *Chunk it backwards for them*: Clearly, some longer pieces of writing will take a long time to write, edit and redraft, and cannot be done in a short amount of time. Learn the skill of chunking backwards – of looking at what you want from the finished piece, and chopping it up into smaller pieces so that your students can complete one at a time.

✓ *Don't expect miracles*: Writing for a long period of time is counterproductive. Enthusiasm flags, exhaustion sets in, and the quality of the writing becomes poor. Even though I am a professional writer, I find it impossible to write effectively for much more than half an hour before taking a break. Set your students a realistic length of time for their writing: 15 minutes is about right to retain focus and energy.

✓ *Keep it fresh*: Give your students regular breaks when they are writing – after writing for about 15 minutes give them a five-minute break to refresh themselves. This time could be used to discuss samples of the work so far, or for the students to chat with a partner about their writing.

✓ *Develop their concentration*: Good concentration is important when writing, especially if you have to write for any length of time (for instance in an exam). This self-discipline and focus is something that many students seem to lack. You can help your students develop their concentration by using the focus activities described in this chapter on pp. 72–73.

✓ *Give them a test*: As exam time approaches, students often become much more focused in their work. We tend to offer our classes exam practice in the run-up to national tests and exams, but there is no need to restrict tests to these times alone. A test also offers the teacher a chance for a 'lesson off', although do stagger the setting of tests to allow for the additional marking.

✓ *Give them a deadline*: In a similar vein, deadlines can work wonders for the unmotivated writer. The closer a submission date for a book or article gets, the more miraculously motivated I seem to become. Utilize the same approach with your students.

✓ *Use unusual motivators*: In my experience, students are always motivated by unusual or imaginative resources or teaching strategies. When approaching work on the Shakespeare play *Romeo and Juliet*, an excellent motivator I have used is to set up the story as a crimescene investigation. The students then work as police officers to examine the evidence and interview witnesses.

Getting them writing properly

As well as having to deal with students who won't write at all, you will also find yourself dealing with those students who produce plenty of writing, but whose work is illegible, or has no punctuation, or doesn't make any sense. Here are some thoughts about getting your students to write in a meaningful and worthwhile way.

✓ *Show them why writing properly is important*: In order to communicate with our readers, our writing must be legible, clear and accurate. Demonstrate this to your class by using the following exercise. Ask your students to write down a short message, but with the wrong hand (i.e. the right-handed students write with their left hand, and vice versa). When they have finished, get them to swap with a partner for translation, and discuss the difficulties of reading and understanding.

✓ *Show them examples of 'incorrect' writing*: Looking at a piece of writing that is 'incorrect' demonstrates the difficulties this creates for the reader. Take a section of text and Tippex out all the punctuation. Study the result to show your students how difficult it is to read without correct punctuation.

✓ *Share the work with the class*: Encourage your students to share, and to mark, each other's work. When students know that their peers will be reading a piece of writing, they tend to take care over it. In addition, they start to get a sense of the type and quality of work that others are producing. (Be careful not to demotivate the very weakest students when using this technique.)

✓ *Share the work across the school*: Share writing across year groups as well – this works well in both the primary and the secondary school. Show a fantastic essay from a couple of years ago to your GCSE group, or get your Year 6 students to write letters to their Year 2 counterparts.

✓ *Ask them to read their writing back to you*: Some weaker writers finish a piece of work quickly, but don't bother to read it through (perhaps for fear of what they might see). When students bring you pieces of writing that are illegible, or poorly punctuated, ask them to read their work back to you. The ensuing struggle should help them realize the vital importance of writing 'properly'.

A reason to write

Often, writing in school is guided by the teacher: 'I want you to write a review of the story we've been reading', or 'I'd like you to write up this science experiment for homework'. The piece of writing produced is then judged and graded by the teacher. Obviously this is necessary if we are to fulfil curriculum requirements and assess our students. However, it does mean that writing can come to seem like a chore and not a choice.

Here are some ideas for giving your students 'a reason to write'.

✓ *Relate the writing to their own lives:* The vast majority of your students will regularly use text-messaging on their mobile phones, so why not bring this form of communication into the classroom? Text messages also offer a very interesting insight into the way that language develops and adapts to suit its medium. You could:
  – Get your students to write a text message dictionary (ask them not to include any rude terms that they know).
  – Ask them to write a story using text-message abbreviations.
  – Buy a cheap phone, and give out the number to your class. They can then text you questions about a topic or feedback on a lesson.
✓ *Make the writing fun*: Find ways to make writing both fun and educational at the same time. Think laterally – how could I approach this task in an unusual, humorous or imaginative way? For instance, students are often asked to 'write about yourself' as an introductory activity. A novel approach to this task is to ask your students to write their own obituary (including details of the horrific way in which they died). This gruesome idea captures their attention and offers an unusual way into a familiar topic.
✓ *Give them an inspiration to write*: Get your students inspired by the use of imaginative resources or unusual ideas. Create 'fictions' for the class, for instance that they are 'television executives' developing a documentary. Use hands-on resources to make your lessons multi-sensory and inspirational.
✓ *Use a group project*: Group projects allow each student more of a choice in the form and style of writing they are going to do, depending on

their strengths or interests. If you offer a fairly wide choice of subjects for the project, each group can make their selection based on personal enjoyment and interest.

✓ *Set up a competition*: A writing competition is a wonderful motivator for student writing. In my first teaching post I had great fun setting up a whole-school poetry competition, publishing the winning entries in a booklet and selling it to parents. This idea would work across the curriculum – a competition for the best history or science project, or for the best biography of a well-known sportsman or woman in PE. Ask your school to fund small prizes such as book tokens to reward the winners. Publish the best entries in a pamphlet to celebrate the students' achievements and make them feel like 'real' writers. Keep an eye out for online competitions as well.

✓ *Make the writing 'real'*: Writing at school can often feel rather contrived. Aim to make it real – to give it a genuine reason for taking place. Get your students to write an email or a letter to an author whose work they love; encourage them to write to a local or national newspaper to complain about an issue of importance. If they are lucky enough to receive replies to their letters, this will give them added encouragement and motivation.

Pots of perfection

I love this idea, which you can use to inspire and motivate students of pretty much any age. The teacher prepares a number of small pots, with lots of miniature items in them, each themed around a different topic, character type, genre, or other idea. There's no right or wrong – be as creative as you like with what you choose to put in your pots.

The students use the pots to provide them with inspiration for their writing – to give them a reason to write and an inspiration to get going. The contents of the pot give them a multisensory, interactive, resource-based starting point. The writing they do can take many different forms. For instance, a story, some poetry, the script for an animation, a cartoon, a character study.

Here are some suggestions about what could be in your pots:

✓ pirate pot: small pirate characters, parrot toy, pieces of eight (gold chocolate coins), a mini treasure map, a toy ship

✓ seaside pot: a selection of shells, some sand, a piece of seaweed, toy creatures from under the sea
✓ Three Little Pigs pot: three small plastic pig toys, some pieces of straw, some twigs, some 'bricks' (these could be made out of clay or Plasticine), a cooking pot
✓ crime genre pot: fake blood, pack of playing cards, map with mysterious markings on it, foreign coins, suspicious-looking white powder, plastic gloves.

An atmosphere for writing

Aim to create a 'mood' in your classroom, in which writing takes place naturally, and in which your students feel relaxed. This could involve building an atmosphere to inspire your students or simply providing a quiet, positive place in which they can work.

Here are some tips on how you can do this:

✓ *Set the boundaries for written work*: Right from the start, set boundaries for how written work takes place in your lessons. You might feel that writing should always be done in silence, or that a low level of talk is acceptable. Perhaps your students write best when listening to music. Talk to your classes about their preferred atmosphere for writing, negotiating the boundaries with them.

✓ *Think about your classroom set-up*: Create a 'comfort zone' for writing, an environment in which environmental factors do not interfere with the writing process. Try to make sure that your students have room on their desks and are not constantly banging elbows with the person sitting next to them. Think about the levels of heat and light in your room, and how these might affect their writing. In the primary classroom, consider allocating a 'free writing' desk, where the children can write freely, without concerns about form or technique.

✓ *Create a dramatic atmosphere*: An inspiring or dramatic atmosphere is great for motivating students. Set the mood for writing a ghost story by blacking out the classroom and sharing some ghost stories with your class by torchlight. Take it one step further by playing a soundtrack of howling wind and creepy night creatures.

✓ *Use a variety of inspirations*: Think about unusual resources for inspiration: music, pictures, objects, etc. can all help create an atmosphere.

Aim to use a prop of some sort in every lesson, to inspire your students and engage their interest in the lesson. To give just one example, show the class a 'magical' box, and tell your students that it is locked shut, and cannot be opened (except by the right spell, of course!). The students could then write about what they imagine is inside the box, and create a spell to open it.

Warm-up exercises

Just as pianists play scales to warm up their fingers, or dancers do stretches to warm up their bodies, so writers need to 'warm up' before they begin work. The warm-ups described below cover both the physical and mental aspects of writing.

✓ *Finger exercises*: Some students suffer from cramp in their hands when writing for long periods of time. This may be the result of a poor writing technique, or of tension or weakness within the hands. Help your students overcome this by using physical warm-ups before you start written work. These finger exercises are also fun! Here is just one example, but there are plenty more that you can do. See Chapter 1 for some more suggestions, or ask any pianists at your school. Get your students to raise their hands in the air, palms away from their body. Now tell them to clench their fists tight, then spread their fingers as wide as possible, feeling the stretch in their palms. Repeat this several times.

✓ *Group brainstorm*: Many teachers use a brainstorm to begin a topic as a matter of course, and this technique does provide an excellent intellectual warm-up activity. Gather together your students' ideas and note them on the board. This helps develop confidence in the less able, giving them some ideas to include in their writing. It also helps the more able to exercise their brains and decide exactly what they already know. Brainstorming is also a vital technique when planning longer pieces of writing such as essays.

✓ *Individual brainstorm*: Turn the simple brainstorm into a competitive style warm-up. Tell the students that you are going to give them a word or phrase ('blue', 'magic', 'the house of horror'). When you say 'go', they have two minutes to write down as many words as they possibly can, inspired by that word or phrase. The winner is the student with the most words.

✓ *Collaborative writing*: This is a fun way to warm up for a story-writing activity. Give the students a single sheet of paper, asking them to write the first sentence of a story on the top line. When they have done this, they pass the paper on to the next student, who writes the next line of the story, then folds the paper down so that only the sentence that they have written is visible. The collaborative stories written in this way are often very amusing.

✓ *Picturing a story*: Again, this provides a good warm-up to a story-writing activity. It also provides a useful focus for students who tend to 'dive into' their writing without thinking about it first. Ask your students to close their eyes and to picture the story in their head, as though they are running a film. You could tell them a story, or they could come up with ideas of their own, perhaps based on a particular topic that you're going to be studying.

Focus exercises

The following 'focus exercises' will help your students develop the vital skills of self-discipline and concentration. They also provide good warm-ups for a writing session. They are based on drama exercises, but most should prove suitable for teachers in any curriculum subject. Some need an open space, while others can be used in a normal classroom setting. These focus exercises are extremely popular with children and young people of all ages.

✓ *Hypnosis*: This exercise requires the students to focus on one thing for a length of time – the basic requirement for concentration. Demonstrate the exercise first by asking a student to come to the front of the class to be 'hypnotized' by you.
   - Tell the student that when you click your fingers she will be 'under your power'.
   - Hold your palm up so that it is level with her face, a short distance away (about 10 cm).
   - Once the student is 'under your power', she must follow you wherever you go, keeping her face at exactly the same distance from your hand.
   - Move your hand around slowly, up and down, side to side, down to the floor, and so on.
   - If you are brave, after demonstrating the exercise you can let the volunteer hypnotize you in return.
   - Get the whole class to do the exercise, working in pairs.

✓ *Count down*: Again, this exercise helps set a 'focus' for your students. They should shut their eyes, and then count backwards from 50 to zero. When they reach zero, they can open their eyes and prepare to write.

✓ *Mental spelling*: Ask your students to close their eyes, and then spell a word or words backwards in their heads. For instance, you could start by asking them to spell their full names, then move on to key words related to the subject being studied.

✓ *Listening*: This is a very simple exercise to set a calm atmosphere before writing begins. Ask your children to close their eyes and simply listen to see what they can hear. At first, they could focus on sounds within the classroom, gradually moving out to sounds in the corridors, and around the school.

✓ *Puppets*: This drama exercise develops the skills of concentration, cooperation and coordination. Again, you could demonstrate it using a student volunteer.

  – One person is the 'puppet-master', the other the puppet.
  – The puppet-master moves his puppet around through the use of invisible strings, keeping his hand at a short distance from the part of the body he is moving.
  – The strings can be attached to the hands, feet, elbows and knees.
  – Alternatively, for an even higher level of focus, there could be strings on each of the fingers, on the head, and so on.

Putting the pleasure back into writing

The contrived nature of much writing in schools means that our students learn to see writing as part of the toil of the school day, rather than something that they might choose to do. We need to show them that it is possible to gain pleasure from writing, or to use it for self-expression. Here are some ideas about how you might do this.

✓ *Have a 'free writing' session*: On occasions give your students the chance to write purely for pleasure. Offer them a totally free choice of form and style – they can write about whatever they want, in any style or form they wish. During this session technique is unimportant – you are not going to be assessing what they write. Some students might choose to write notes to each other, others to write an article about their favourite pop group. Rather than marking the results, ask your class to share their work by reading it out loud. Talk to them about their reasons for choosing a particular form and subject and why it appeals to them. This will help you learn more about your students' interests – information that you can put to good use when planning your lessons.

✓ *Offer valuable rewards for good writing*: Depending on what motivates your students, whether it is merit marks or Mars bars, use these rewards to encourage good writing. The reward of seeing their work published can be a huge factor in giving your students pleasure from writing. There are many websites that publish student work – see the companion website for details. Alternatively, set up a page on a school website to show off the best writing.

✓ *Display good written work*: Displaying good pieces of writing will help motivate your students. Remember to display the work of your less able as well as your more able students. If you feel it is necessary, get the student to redraft or type up a piece of work to correct spelling errors before displaying it. See the final chapter of this book – Chapter 15 – for some ideas about imaginative ways to display your students' writing.

✓ *Encourage keen writers*: There are probably students in your class who write for pleasure outside of school time, although you are not aware of it. My own students have shown me examples of poetry, novels and autobiographies, asking for my thoughts on what they have done. Show your students that you are interested in any writing that they do, not just in the class assignments that you set.

The teacher as writer

A great way to motivate your students is for them to see you, their teacher, as a writer. Your skill in modelling activities for the class can also help them learn about the processes involved in writing. Your students see you as a writer when you scribble notes on the classroom whiteboard, when you write evaluative comments on their work, when you create sample texts for them to analyse.

Your students will pick up on how you personally feel about doing writing in your classroom. Do you communicate a sense that it's an exciting part of your role, one that you enjoy and feel confident about? Or do you subconsciously let your students know that you lack confidence in modelling writing in front of an audience, or that you have concerns about your presentation or spelling? Your students will quickly pick up on your own emotional attitudes to writing. Clearly, if you're an English teacher, you have chosen to teach this subject and I'm sure you feel very positive about it. But if you're teaching literacy at primary level, you may be less certain and confident about your own writing. Take care not to communicate this to your class.

At the same time, don't be afraid to show your students that you can't always find the right word straight away, or that sometimes you need to rewrite a piece, to make sure you communicate what you meant. These are all features of being a writer – talk about them with your students as you experience them. To show your class that you are a writer, as well as a teacher, make sure that you:

✓ *Do it with them*: When you set an activity, don't always head off round the class to see what the students are doing. Sometimes give yourself permission to sit down and write with your students. This is particularly effective when you're asking students to take a risk in their writing.

✓ *Articulate the process*: When you're modelling an exercise on the whiteboard, show that writing is an active process, where decisions are constantly being made. Comment on your writing as it takes place. Talk about the thoughts that go through your head: how should I structure this, where should I put that idea, which words should I use? Ah, I need to chuck this bit away, or oh, that's a good bit isn't it?

✓ *Involve your students*: Ask for your students' ideas and involve them in the act of decision making. Allow them to contribute, either orally or by coming up to the board and writing down their ideas.

✓ *Create a dialogue*: Use writing to set up a dialogue with your students. Write a series of questions on a piece of completed writing, and ask the students to reply to your queries.

✓ *Communicate through writing*: When you first meet a class, get them to write you a letter telling you all about themselves. In return, write a postcard, letter or email to each of your students about their writing and about their individual targets for improvement. Then get them to answer your letter, setting some additional targets of their own. This can and should become an ongoing process of discussion through writing.

I'm often asked by teachers who are would-be authors, how to go about getting published and making some money from their writing. For some ideas about how teachers can write professionally, or for their own enjoyment, see the companion website.

Part 2

Writing across the Curriculum

5

Writing in All the Subjects

The school of hard knocks is an accelerated curriculum.

Menander of Athens

Of course, writing takes place in every part of the curriculum, and this chapter focuses on approaches to writing in different curriculum areas. You'll find general ideas for motivating your writers in all the subjects, and specific approaches for individual curriculum areas. Whatever subject in the curriculum you teach, your students will use writing for key skills such as planning, selecting and presenting information, problem solving, decision making, reporting, explaining, essay writing, and so on.

You can find a list of subject-specific vocabulary on the companion website.

Many of the ideas that I give in this chapter are linked by their use of imaginative approaches. By making writing activities really creative and engaging for students, you will be rewarded with high levels of motivation. Look for the links between a subject and the wider world – make writing activities feel real and relevant. Link the subjects together as well, teaching in a cross-curricular way whenever you can. Show your students that these are not isolated subject areas, but part of a whole. Towards the end of this chapter you'll find some ideas for cross-curricular writing projects which will help you do just that.

Writing in practical subjects

It is often a particular challenge to teach writing in those subjects which are partly or mainly practical. Be aware of the potential difficulties, and think ahead to overcome them. The issues you might encounter could include:

✘ *Negative attitudes to the writing*: Some students feel hard done by when asked to write in practical subjects. This can lead to conflict and bad feelings. Those students who particularly enjoy practical work are often the least able and the poorly behaved, who find it hard to succeed elsewhere in the curriculum. When the teacher asks for written work this seems tantamount to ruining their only chance of success.

✗ *Negative attitudes to the subject*: Other students may have a negative attitude towards the subject itself, viewing it as a poor relation to the core curriculum of English, maths and science. These subject-related attitudes come about for a range of reasons, particularly the lack of statutory exams in these areas and parental attitudes about which school subjects are most important.

✗ *Poor-quality writing/poor behaviour*: If the students do not view the writing as an integral part of the lesson, the teacher might find that they produce only poor-quality work. Similarly, the negative attitudes of some students might mean they start to misbehave when they are asked to write.

✗ *'Writing up' rather than writing about*: Often, written tasks are all about 'writing up' what has been done in a practical lesson. Although recording the learning will form an important part of a subject, leave room for creative activities as well. Even if the information being recorded is factual, the form used could be creative (for instance, writing up a science report as a recipe).

✗ *Finding a writing place or space*: If you're teaching in an open space such as a drama studio or a gym, there may well be problems finding a suitable place or space to write. If you have to move the whole class into a classroom to write at desks, this can cause problems: wasted lesson time, resentment from the class about not doing practical learning.

✗ *Equipment, materials and resources*: Students who turn up expecting a practical lesson might not bring writing equipment or materials with them. You need to decide whether the students should be given exercise books, or whether they will write on loose paper (with the consequent potential for losing work).

✗ *Storing and accessing the writing*: There are also questions to be asked about how and where the work is going to be stored. If it is kept in an area away from the normal teaching space, this can cause problems of access.

Of course, there are lots of ways in which the teacher can overcome all these problems. Many of the tips given below come as a direct result of my experiences when incorporating writing tasks into a practical subject (drama).

✓ *Make writing time part of the routine*: If you need to incorporate writing into a practical lesson, then set up writing time as part of the routine right from the word go. Clarify exactly where, when and how writing will take place, both in your own mind and for your students.

✓ *Set clear expectations*: Make your expectations clear – the standard of work required, the equipment that must be brought, and so on. Explain the percentage of lesson time that will be taken up by writing, and make it clear that practical tasks will only be done if the writing is taken seriously as well.

✓ *Make writing an integral part of the work*: Steer clear of too many 'writing-up' style activities. Instead, make sure the writing goes hand-in-hand with what you do in the practical lessons, feeding into or out of the work and having a clear sense of purpose.

✓ *Review the lesson in writing*: A good way of integrating writing into practical work is to use written reviews at the end of the lesson. Give your students a clear frame or structure for their reviews to ensure that they write good quality pieces.

✓ *Use written homework tasks*: If you have serious problems finding somewhere to write in your practical lessons, consider setting written tasks as homework instead. Homework might include background research, preparation for the next lesson, gathering written texts to refer to, and so on.

✓ *Sort out your materials*: Get your writing materials sorted out from the start of the year, introducing these to the students and sorting out any storage issues. If you do not have access to desks, rather than trooping your whole class halfway across the school, consider using a set of clipboards. If your class are going to write on loose paper, then ensure that each student has a folder in which to keep their work.

Motivation across the curriculum

Whatever subject or subjects you teach, when you want your students to write there are some proactive approaches you can take to ensure good levels of motivation.

To keep your students motivated:

✓ Keep it topical – use current news, TV, celebrities, fads and crazes.
✓ Keep it real – stay as close to 'real life' as you can to show a clear link between school and the real world.

✓ Be authentic – give your students real-life situations and materials to inspire their writing.
✓ Use 'games' – word searches, quizzes, competitions all keep motivation high.
✓ Ensure success – for the very weak writers, give tasks that allow them to succeed, such as 'filling in the blanks'.
✓ Use 'frames' – give an outline structure for more complex pieces of writing.
✓ Keep it active – taking an active part in the lesson keeps your students interested and helps them learn.
✓ Make it visually attractive – ask your students to present their writing in an appealing way, and give them attractive materials with which to work.
✓ Use fictional approaches – get your students to play characters, by using role plays or the 'role of the expert'.

Art and design

The vast majority of work in art and design involves the use of different visual media. The students learn to communicate what they see, feel or think through using colour, form, texture, pattern, different materials and processes, rather than via the written word. However, there will still be a place for writing, perhaps to:

– form an integral part of the design process (see the lesson ideas below)
– write reviews of their own work, or that of others
– brainstorm ideas for their art/design
– find starting points, for instance from stories or poems
– make notes on the success of different ideas, methods and approaches.

Lesson ideas
✓ Write and illustrate an animal story, using the book *Elmer the Elephant* as a starting point.
✓ Learn to write calligraphy, hieroglyphics or Chinese characters.
✓ Explore different fonts (perhaps on a computer) and examine the varying effects and moods that these give.
✓ Create sculptures of different letters or words.
✓ Set up a whole class 'art exhibition', then make posters to advertise this and write a newspaper review in response.
✓ Design and write postcards in response to work on art from different cultures.

Lesson outline – Packaging
The children examine different examples of packaging, looking at the visual impact of both images and language. They move on to invent a new chocolate bar, cereal, toy, etc. and then design and create the packaging that goes with it, including suitable wording and experimenting with different font styles. As an extension, they create posters or television adverts to promote their new product.

Citizenship

This fairly new area of the curriculum offers lots of potential for imaginative and engaging written activities. The students might:

- write to express a personal opinion – 'What makes a good citizen?'
- examine other people's experiences and views through writing
- make notes from research and use of ICT
- explore the media – writing in different styles, to affect the reader's opinion
- write for a real purpose – for example, to help with voluntary groups or community activities.

Lesson ideas

✓ Write a leaflet to explain the work done by a local community group, or a group within the school, and to encourage new volunteers to join in.

✓ Write a letter to the local newspaper to express an opinion on a local issue.

✓ Set up an election within the school – ask the students to write individual manifestos to outline their beliefs and policies, for election to a school council.

✓ Look at crime and punishment – set up a whole-class trial for different crimes, write opening and closing arguments for the defence and prosecution.

Lesson outline – The media – GM Foods
Examine the controversy surrounding recent developments in genetically modified farming. Study some examples of media responses to the GM issue, identifying how use of language can affect public opinion. Divide the class into groups, giving each group a type of media (broadsheet newspaper, tabloid newspaper, publicly funded radio station, TV advert) and a focus either 'for' or 'against' this issue. Ask the students to write a report or script using this specific viewpoint and trying to persuade their audience to agree with their opinions.

Design and technology (DT)

Within a design and technology lesson, you'll find a variety of different writing forms and styles: from the initial, scribbled ideas to a finished design folder with detailed notes, work and drawings. Many of the skills developed in DT lessons tie in closely to those skills required for effective writing. The students will:

– plan and sequence steps and ideas
– write design briefs
– list what a design will achieve
– generate, develop and structure ideas
– explain clearly what a product will do
– have a sense of audience – who will use the product, how it should look
– create realistic working schedules, prioritizing and sticking to deadlines
– evaluate how well an idea has worked
– identify criteria to judge the quality of a piece.

Lesson ideas
✓ Write instructions for and then build a monster truck.
✓ Write a list of ten products that could be made using an empty plastic bottle.
✓ Design and create new packaging for a familiar product (e.g. Coca-Cola), including the design of the new text style and language.
✓ Create posters or leaflets to promote safety awareness in DT.

✓ Take an existing product, for instance a bird box, and brainstorm new ideas about how it might be designed.

✓ Write a catalogue of new products in a specific area, for instance tools and other items for the garden.

✓ Make a new toy for children, and write a storybook to accompany it – for example, a toy clock and a book about telling the time.

Lesson outline – Castaway

Tell the class that they are going to be 'castaway' on a desert island. They must chose five essential items to take with them. For each item, they should write a list of potential uses and the reasons why they would want to take this particular thing. Once the class has been 'castaway', give out a series of problems that must be solved, using only the chosen items and any natural materials that they might find. Your problems could include: build and start a fire; open a coconut for food; catch fish; build a shelter; survive a storm; build a raft to escape.

Geography

Geography offers some really wonderful opportunities for interesting and exciting written tasks. Many of the techniques used in geography lessons fall closely in line with the key skills and approaches that effective writers must develop.

Your students will learn:

– to ask and answer questions about people, places and environments
– investigation and problem-solving skills
– to view issues from different perspectives – understanding and resolving these issues
– to explore their place in the world – what values, rights and responsibilities they have
– to make and record observations
– to collect and analyse data and information
– to develop their own opinions and express their views
– to work with secondary sources, such as stories and other texts
– to find, recognize and explain patterns
– to undertake investigations – gather views and evidence and come to conclusions
– to communicate in a way that is appropriate to the task and audience.

Lesson ideas

✓ Work as a 'disaster relief team' – researching, planning for and helping out in an area where there has been a natural disaster.

✓ Draw and label a map of an island where 'pirate treasure' is hidden.

✓ Write a tourist brochure and postcards from a country that you're studying.

✓ Work in role as a person who lives in another place or country, then write diary entries to reflect their perspectives and experiences of life.

✓ Write a leaflet entitled 'Welcome to Earth', aimed at aliens from another planet, explaining what Earth's environment is like.

✓ Investigate the impact of transport on the local environment, and write a letter to the local council about ways this could be improved.

Lesson outline – Environmental disaster

The students write the script for a short film about an environmental disaster, for instance the *Exxon Valdez* oil spill, or the more recent BP spill in the Gulf of Mexico. They incorporate extracts from television news reports of the time. They research the subject by writing to organizations such as Greenpeace and BP. The groups act out and video their films, and host a screening for parents.

History

There is huge potential within history lessons for working with a whole variety of written forms. In their History lessons, your students learn to:

– work with chronological order, sequencing and past/present/future tenses
– use a variety of sources of information, including stories and eye-witness accounts
– ask and answer questions
– work with information to recall, prioritize and select
– create structured narratives
– develop substantiated explanations and come to conclusions
– work with words and phrases that relate to the passing of time
– look at different interpretations and the reasons behind them
– select and record relevant information.

Lesson ideas

✓ Work as 'time travellers' to go back to a specific historical event, then research and write a report from the perspective of people at the time.

✓ Write a children's story set in the past, using words and phrases such as 'a long time ago' and 'in the last century'.

✓ Use an artefact to inspire and develop in-role writing, for instance writing diary entries in response to a ration book from the Second World War.

✓ Write a fictional 'school report' on a significant figure from the past.

✓ Write timelines for different time periods – last week, last year, the 20th century, 2000 BC to AD 2000.

✓ Explore the symptoms and effects of the plague, and write 'a doctor's report' about the treatment of the sick.

✓ Write a newspaper story about the Great Fire of London, in tabloid and broadsheet style.

✓ Create an 'agony aunt' column in which problems sent in by historical characters are answered.

Lesson outline – Back in time

Set up your classroom as a village from a particular historical era (for instance the medieval period). The students dress as characters from that time, and are given the jobs that people would have done. You can use this activity to explore living conditions, and how diseases such as malnutrition and the plague could have taken hold as a consequence. Writing that arises from this setting might include diary entries, newspaper reports, 'aged' documents, and so on.

Information and communication technology (ICT)

A great deal of the activities done in ICT lessons involve the use of the written word. You can find more thoughts about writing in the digital age in Chapter 9 of this book.

In their ICT lessons, your students will learn how to:

– use research skills – find relevant information, retrieve it, classify it and check it for accuracy
– interpret, select and organize information effectively
– consider audience needs in terms of content, quality and presentation

- develop and refine ideas and subsequently review them
- investigate and solve problems
- write instructions and create sequences
- ask 'what if' questions
- identify patterns and relationships
- find the best ways of presenting work, e.g. DTP, multimedia.

Lesson ideas

✓ Create a PowerPoint presentation for aliens, with the title 'Welcome to Earth'.

✓ Write for publication on the internet (see Appendix 2 for website addresses).

✓ Create tickets, posters and programmes for a school play.

✓ Write a whole-class 'chain story' using email, with each recipient adding one line to the story.

✓ Plan, design, write and edit a class or school magazine, using a DTP program.

✓ Create frames, templates or macros for different written forms, e.g. letters, recipes, newspaper articles.

Lesson outline – Safety on the net

The students work in groups to develop and make a pamphlet concerning internet safety, aimed at children lower down the school. They analyse their audience's needs, researching pre-existing attitudes to internet usage. They research the topic and audience in detail before starting, making notes about any cases in the media, writing in a way that will suit the projected audience, using effective presentation, and so on. When the pamphlets are completed, they test their pamphlet out on the projected audience and make notes on the responses.

Maths

The language of maths is that of numbers and shapes, and most of the learning that takes place in lessons involves the use of this mathematical language. There are, however, many skills and techniques within the subject of mathematics that feed into, and from, the writing that our students do.

In maths lessons, the students will:

– use intellectual processes, such as logical organization, to structure and break down problems, moving step by step, sorting and classifying
– be precise: specify problems, summarize, check for accuracy
– use questions: 'If … then …', 'What if …?'
– make inferences and deductions, create and examine theories.

Lesson ideas

✓ Role play 'real life' maths problems, e.g. buying items in a shop, writing a shopping list and working out how much they need to spend.

✓ Get your students to write fun and imaginative 'If … then …' questions, for instance 'If each alien from the Planet Zog has three legs and five arms, then how many limbs do 20 aliens from Zog have?'

✓ Create maths-related storybooks to teach counting or shapes to children, and then try these out on a class lower down the school.

✓ Design a maths board game, for instance, where mathematical symbols and shapes must be matched to the correct vocabulary.

Lesson outline – Maths at the match
This idea can be adapted to use with any topic that your students particularly enjoy. Ask the class to write a series of mathematical questions relating to Bob's journey to the football match. These can vary in difficulty depending on the age and ability of the students. For instance: 'If the football match starts at 3 pm, and it takes Bob 1 hour 15 minutes to get there, what time should he leave his house?' For a more able or older class, the question might be: 'If the football match starts at 3 pm, and the train journey to the ground takes 45 minutes, what time must Bob leave if he wants to arrive 20 minutes early?'

Modern foreign languages (MFL)

In MFL the emphasis is increasingly on speaking the target language. However, there is huge potential for developing writing in MFL lessons. Many of the skills practised during MFL lessons are of great value for students' writing in English, as well as in the target language.

In MFL your students learn (in the target language) to:

- develop their knowledge about language itself – exploring aspects such as grammar, expression, structures, tenses, types of word
- adapt writing to suit its context, purpose and audience
- write for real purposes – sending messages by letter or email
- write in a variety of contexts – social, workplace, etc.
- summarize and report, take notes
- write authentic materials – newspapers, magazines, brochures, etc.
- redraft writing to improve accuracy and presentation
- write signs, labels, instructions.

Lesson ideas

✓ Write emails or letters to a pen pal in a country where the target language is spoken (see Appendix 2 for website addresses).

✓ Create magazines on specific topics in the target language, e.g. a pop magazine in French, a sports magazine in German.

✓ Write a short language course for young children in the target language, with fun games and activities, and colourful presentation.

✓ Take a fictional 'plane journey' (the teacher lines the desks up in rows and pretends to be an air steward) and then make and write postcards home.

✓ Read recipe books and then write recipes in the target language for delicious dishes.

✓ Role play in various situations – the shop, the office – write in character during the role play, or write up a script of the scene.

Lesson outline – The footballer's assistant (Spanish)
This lesson uses the 'role of the expert' (see p. 157) to ensure full involvement and motivation from the students. The students work as personal assistants to a famous figure who has recently moved to work overseas. They must help him plan for his move by completing a variety of tasks, including: finding and listing possible accommodation, creating a booklet of 'key phrases' in Spanish for him to learn, giving details of cultural events, local restaurants and so on.

Music

Just as in art, music offers a way for our students to express themselves in a language other than that of words. The majority of activities will involve listening to, exploring and creating, music. However, the written word might be used in a variety of ways, including to:

- brainstorm initial ideas for the focus of a piece of music
- create lyrics for songs or chants
- write about the music of other cultures, both past and present
- reflect on, record and write reviews of what has been achieved in lessons.

Lesson ideas

✓ Explore a range of song lyrics from films, asking the students to write their own lyrics for a new or current movie.

✓ Bring in an unusual object, such as a coconut, then get the class to brainstorm ideas about how this might be used as an inspiration for a piece of music.

✓ Look at reviews in a variety of music magazines; use these as a basis for writing a review of a piece of music created in class.

✓ Create a rhyming dictionary, giving lists of rhymes for words, to use when writing song lyrics.

✓ Write the lyrics and music for a new and up-to-date school song, perhaps based around the school motto.

Lesson outline – Protest music

The students work in-role as the guests and audience on a chat show: the topic of this week's show is 'Music – can it make a difference?' The guests are famous singers/musicians past and present, including protest singers such as Bob Marley and Billy Bragg, and Bob Dylan. Members of the audience question them about what their music is for and whether it can make a difference to people's lives. The class moves on to look at examples of different protest lyrics and to write their own protest songs.

Personal, social and health education (PSHE)

PSHE offers some wonderful opportunities for writing in a wide range of forms, and for a whole variety of different audiences. Because the subject is very much a study of themselves and their relationship with the world, the students tend to view it as being real and relevant to their lives. The writing that the students do might be based on a whole range of topics, to include learning how to:

- express their personal likes and dislikes, feelings, opinions and views
- set personal goals and targets for themselves
- look after themselves – health, hygiene, safety
- examine their own behaviour, and that of others
- topical issues – what is right and what is wrong?
- how we might improve or harm our environment
- real choices about areas such as healthy eating, television and money.

Lesson ideas
✓ Design posters and other materials for a 'Stop the bullies' campaign.
✓ Run a 'Save the environment' campaign within the school, including posters to encourage recycling, anti-litter notices, researching local recycling initiatives, etc.
✓ Create a list of 'my personal goals', giving five targets for self-improvement, either within school or at home.
✓ Write a story about where they want to be, and what they want to be doing, in 10, 15 or 20 years' time.
✓ Plan, write and illustrate a book for children called 'My body'.
✓ Write a webpage on road safety for pedestrians, cyclists and drivers.
✓ Write a list of all the things that are good about one of their classmates.
✓ Script a class assembly on a topic such as racism or HIV.
✓ Create a problem page, on which they work as agony aunts and uncles to answer common concerns of children their age.

Lesson outline – *Who Wants to be a Millionaire?*
Start by watching an extract from the TV programme, in which the contestant wins a large sum of money. Now ask your students to imagine what it would be like to have this much money. Tell them to write a list of 10 or twenty things that they would do or buy with the money. Ask them to think carefully about the impact of their choices. Would they share the money, or spend it all themselves? How might other people feel towards them after their win?

Physical education (PE)

While the majority of activities in PE lessons are physical ones, there are areas of the subject that benefit from or require the use of the written word.

Students could use writing to:

- plan and evaluate actions, ideas and performances
- remember sequences or moves or actions
- explain the rules and conventions for different activities
- plan, use and adapt strategies, tactics and compositional ideas
- study the physiological aspects of sport
- explore safety issues.

Lesson ideas

✓ Write a survival booklet giving lists of equipment and safety factors for an orienteering activity.

✓ Create posters or lists of rules concerning safety within PE generally, or within a specific sport.

✓ Write a comic strip to show the correct technique for different moves within a game.

✓ Label the giant outline of a body to show where and how the most common sports injuries occur.

✓ Design a poster or script an advert to encourage people to do more sport.

Lesson outline – Instruction booklet

After learning a new game, such as rounders, basketball or netball, the students write an instruction booklet about the rules and directions for playing the game. To make this activity more engaging, ask them to choose an unusual 'audience' for their writing, such as an alien with three arms. They must alter the rules to fit this unusual player!

Religious education (RE)

There are plenty of opportunities within RE lessons for writing in a variety of forms and for a range of purposes. The use of stories and texts plays an integral role within the subject.

Students might write to:

- consider questions of meaning and purpose in life
- develop knowledge and understanding of different religions
- express, reflect on, analyse and evaluate beliefs
- develop a sense of identity and belonging
- identify puzzling questions, and find answers
- look at the beliefs and cultures of others
- share the celebrations of different faiths.

Lesson ideas
- ✓ Look at the calligraphy in early religious books, and then write a poem or story about your own beliefs, using calligraphy to present it.
- ✓ Make posters, cards or decorations to celebrate a variety of festivals.
- ✓ Consider the role of symbolism within religion – for instance, writing about the symbolic nature of light within different faiths.
- ✓ Write newspaper or magazine articles about key figures within different religions.
- ✓ Update stories from sacred texts, rewriting them within a present-day context.
- ✓ Make a book of religious stories for young children.
- ✓ Write a diary entry from the perspective of a key religious character, at a point when they face a big challenge.

> **Lesson outline – Newspaper article**
> A report on the death of Jesus during a study of early Christianity, as seen in the newspaper *The Jerusalem Echo*. The report includes descriptions of the crucifixion from Roman soldiers, interviews with the followers of Jesus, quotations taken from the Bible, etc.

Science

Science offers plenty of opportunities for our students to develop key writing skills. Although the learning involves lots of practical approaches, even during these activities the students are learning techniques that can feed into and out of their writing.

They will learn how to:

- use precise language and meaning, and take context into account
- ask questions – how, why, what if?
- follow instructions
- work in a logical and coherent way

- explore – make use of the senses
- make comparisons, find patterns and associations
- label and create diagrams
- group, classify and sort by characteristics
- work with lots of different vocabulary, e.g. changing materials – bend, squash, twist, stretch; circulation – heart, blood vessels, pump
- come to conclusions, test explanations.

Lesson ideas

✓ Ask the students to 'imagine you are a ...' (bird, rock, atom, etc.) and to write from this perspective about their experiences and the way that they see the world.

✓ Use nursery rhymes to explore different scientific ideas, for instance 'The Three Little Pigs' to examine building materials. From this they write instructions to make a stable building, diaries of a pig's day, and so on.

✓ Get the class to write a hypothesis based on 'What would happen if ...' Some ideas could be: 'What would happen if wheels were square?' or 'What would happen if there were no clouds?'

✓ Blindfold some volunteers and give them various objects or substances to touch, smell or taste. Ask the class to write about their sensory responses to these different things.

✓ Use a toy as an inspiration for testing different materials. Teddy accidentally gets left behind by his owner, and decides to find his own way home. In his way is a river, and he must work out how to cross it. He tries various different materials to see whether they sink or float, then makes a raft. They write up the story of 'Teddy's Big Adventure'.

Lesson outline – Journey into space

The teacher puts the chairs in the classroom into rows, in the same layout as on an aeroplane. The students are going on a journey into space, in their very own spaceship. As they fly away from the Earth, you introduce the various planets that they travel past (do this on your interactive whiteboard if you have one available). They make a 'logbook' for the spaceship, writing down notes about each planet that they pass. They also send letters home to their families, describing the different planets that they have seen. To make this work more exciting, your spaceship can encounter some asteroids on the way, which hit the spaceship and throw the students about inside.

All together now: cross-curricular writing projects

Of course writing is an activity that takes place across the curriculum, rather than just in English lessons. Remember that writing is not just used to show what you already know, it also provides a very useful tool for working out your thinking on a concept. For instance, you could draw a mind-map to show how the various aspects of a topic link together.

Teachers and schools need to show students how and why writing is important right across the curriculum – all the different applications and forms it takes. Creating cross-curricular projects is one great way to show writing in all its myriad uses. The natural connections between subjects can be used and enjoyed, to make learning feel relevant and real for the students.

Organizing cross-curricular learning

The term 'creative curriculum' is commonly used to describe cross-curricular learning; you might also hear it referred to as a 'skills-based' curriculum. The important thing is seen to be the links between subjects and the skills and approaches that are commonly used. Activities are based around a central theme (the Romans, Survival, Habitats) and the students learn about different subjects under this umbrella.

Depending on the age group you teach, the type of school where you work, and the educational philosophy of your head teacher, your cross-curricular learning might happen:

- all the time, for instance as a basis for students' learning in subjects such as English, art and the humanities
- one day per week or per fortnight, perhaps on a 'creative Friday'
- during longer lessons (often two hours or more) where teachers work in an interdisciplinary way
- with larger than normal groups or classes, and with two or more teachers team teaching the group
- with teachers from different subjects being used as 'experts' and dropping in on lessons to give advice or to present information and ideas
- during a 'collapse day' (a day where the normal timetable is 'collapsed') around a central theme; this day could involve a single year group, a key stage, or even the whole school.

Good practice for cross-curricular teaching

A large percentage of school time is devoted to teaching individual subjects. This means that, when taking a cross-curricular approach, it's essential to plan and organize resources etc. carefully ahead of time.

✓ Devote sufficient time for teachers to meet and discuss the appropriate content and skills that might be covered. How do the skills sets match up between the different subjects?

✓ Involve teachers who specialize in the different subjects you intend to deliver. This will ensure that your project has sufficient rigour, and covers the relevant curriculum areas in plenty of depth.

✓ Give your students a sense of ownership, by allowing them input into the theme you choose to cover, or the direction in which that theme will be approached.

✓ Encourage your students to work out the questions that they want answered during the course of the project.

✓ Use a 'working wall' display to track progress during the project – this is a display that gets added to as the learning goes on.

✓ Consider how you are going to resource the project – choose high-quality, imaginative resources that will inspire your students.

✓ Think of people as a resource – not just staff but also any parents who have specialist expertise around this particular area.

✓ Make use of targets to keep the project on track. Encourage students to map out their time and make the best use of it.

✓ Consider working towards a finished 'end result' or 'product' during the course of the project.

✓ Have clear objectives about what the topic will achieve, and the kinds of writing that will be done.

Creative ideas for cross-curricular writing projects

Once you have your central theme in place, and the bulk of the planning has been done, you can set your students going on the topic. Use some or all of the creative approaches below.

✓ Launch your topic at an assembly, to show its importance and to start with a 'bang'.

✓ Get your students to start by writing – why is this subject or topic important, what do they want to know about it?

✓ Consider giving journals to the students, so that they can record their ideas and thinking along the way. Encourage them to see these as 'working notebooks', which they can fill with scribbles, doodles, scraps of text or photos.

✓ Use questions to inspire their curiosity and get them started – find the 'central questions' within your topic area.

✓ Use your expertise as teachers to input advice on appropriate forms for writing, the best approaches to try, the kind of techniques to use, the factual information required, and so on.

✓ Display the texts your students create in unusual ways – on the ceiling, under tables, as a wall hanging.

✓ Use multimedia approaches – take photos to record information and ideas as well as writing text.

✓ Launch a blog to document the project, and use virtual learning environments such as Moodle to bring all the strands together.

✓ Go on a field trip – take along some 'experts' with you to give input – authors, scientists, engineers.

✓ Use interviews and questionnaires to gather information on your topic.

6

Essay Writing

Mighty oaks from little acorns grow.

Proverb

For many students, essay writing retains a mystique: the sense that there must be some 'magic' involved in creating this particular form of writing. But this is untrue. The skills and techniques used in *all* forms of writing can be learned. It just needs the skilful teacher to break down the steps and the processes, so that they are laid bare for the learners. In this chapter I give you lots of ideas about how to demystify essay writing for your students – to make it as simple, accessible and straightforward for them as possible. You'll find a detailed explanation of the 'SEED' technique – a four-step essay-writing process which has proved successful for me in teaching essay writing to students of all abilities. By using this technique, your students can learn to 'grow' their own essay, paragraph by paragraph, from that first seed of an idea.

Some basic tips

Before we look in detail at the techniques involved in writing an essay, let's begin with some basic tips on teaching essay writing. I have divided these up into strategies for the teacher and for the students.

Tips for the teacher

When it comes to writing essays, practise really does make perfect. It will help your students a great deal if you:

✓ go through lots and lots of sample questions with your classes
✓ show them the techniques involved by articulating the process of writing as you work through these questions together
✓ share as many previous exam questions as you can find – demystify the kind of topics they will be asked to write essays about

✓ demonstrate and model the use of planning brainstorms (see p. 103) for essay writing and also for revision purposes
✓ go through the marking criteria to show them how to gain maximum marks in their exams
✓ give them examples of well-written essays, either from previous students or samples that you have written yourself
✓ share the tips given throughout this book about different writing techniques.

There is no need for your students to write out a full essay every time they look at a practice question. You can make better use of time by sometimes getting them to write out a series of plans to show how they would answer the question in full in an exam.

Tips for the student

The points given below cover those areas where I see my students make frequent mistakes. These strategies need to be reiterated over and again: essay writing is a complex business and it takes time to get it right.

✓ *Answer the question*: Your students absolutely must learn to do this. An essay that does not answer the question that has been asked might as well not have been written at all. Right from the start, drum this point into your students.
✓ *Use the correct tense*: For most of the time, essays should be written in the present tense, as though describing something (for instance, an event in a novel) that is happening in the current moment. One exception to this is when recounting factual events from the past.
✓ *Avoid mixing tenses*: Unless it is intentional, tell your students to stick to one tense in their essays. Again, the exception to this might come in an essay where events from the past are explained, for instance in history.
✓ *Avoid slang*: Essays should be written in Standard English, and slang should not be used unless in direct quotation from a text.
✓ *Avoid abbreviations*: They should also avoid abbreviations such as 'I'd' or 'it's', because they make the essay style sound too informal.
✓ *Use a simple (but formal) style*: Encourage your students to use clear and simple language and expression. Although the style should be formal, students can sometimes take this too far in an attempt to sound 'clever'. Discourage them from using overly complicated language – a simply written essay allows the ideas to shine through.
✓ *Don't be afraid of a personal reaction*: There is often scope within essay questions for some type of personal comment. Teach your students to

keep an eye out for the chance to input their own ideas – this might be indicated by a question that says 'Comment on your own feelings about/opinion of …'

✓ *Give an interpretation of the evidence*: Advise your students to suggest, rather than insist on, the points they make in an essay. This allows scope to introduce unusual ideas, or to make comments about which there is some disagreement or controversy. For instance, starting a point by saying: 'It is possible that …' or 'One potential interpretation of this is …'

✓ *Take care with the 'royal we'*: Unless it is handled with care, the 'royal we' can make the style of an essay seem rather pompous or self-satisfied, especially when used by younger students. There is also the danger that 'we' statements seem overly confident, rather than interpretive (a problem if the statements are incorrect!). It is simple to minimize the use of 'we': instead of writing 'We can see that …' your students say 'It could be argued that …'

Planning an essay

When planning an essay, it works well for students to use a series of brainstorms, as described in Chapter 3 (p. 59). Each brainstorm should cover the contents of one paragraph, with perhaps four or five different points that are going to be included, and any quotations or facts that the student is planning to discuss. Using brainstorms in this way to plan an essay has a number of advantages:

✓ *Time efficiency*: This method offers a quick way of giving overall structure to the piece, and consequently is particularly useful in exams. Some students view time spent planning as 'wasted time', especially when they are under pressure in an exam. With practice your students will find that using this planning method allows them to write essays more quickly and effectively.

✓ *Sticking to the point*: Having a single 'main idea' at the centre of each brainstorm helps your students stick to the point they are making within each paragraph.

✓ *Creating a structure*: Each brainstorm should provide enough material for a single paragraph. This approach helps your students remember to paragraph their essays. It also allows them to play around with the structure of the piece before starting to write, for instance changing the order in which they introduce each new paragraph/idea.

✓ *Introduction and conclusion*: It is hard to decide exactly what you are going to say in an introduction or conclusion before an essay has actually been written. I always write the introduction to my books after I've finished writing them! By leaving a blank brainstorm at the start and end of their plan, the students can work out the overall structure and focus of their essay, then complete the plan by filling in the introduction and conclusion brainstorms at the end.

✓ *Adding in ideas*: Creating a series of brainstorms for a plan allows some flexibility if the student comes up with new ideas during the course of writing the essay, as often happens. These ideas can easily be slotted into the overall structure by adding them to the brainstorms.

✓ *Demonstrating their ideas*: If a student runs out of time when writing an examination essay, the examiner may take their planning into account when she marks the essay. The brainstorm plan gives a clear indication of what the student was planning to write, had he not run out of time.

You can see an example of this planning method in Figure 6.1. I have based the essay plan on the generalized question used in Chapter 3 (Figure 3.1), 'What role does technology play in your life?'

Answering the question

Stress over and over to your students that they must answer the question they have been asked. In both examination and coursework essays, they will only gain marks for answering the question, so it is vital that they learn how to do this. Share the following strategies for 'answering the question' with your classes:

✓ *Read the questions first and last*: In an exam where the students are asked to comment on a piece of text, the very first thing they should do is to read the questions they will be required to answer afterwards. This should be done before they read the passage, as well as after. Doing this helps them focus on finding the relevant information as they read.

✓ *Use the question to answer the question*: This technique helps your students stick to the question, and it is also useful for those who have trouble getting started in exams. I have found it particularly helpful for lower secondary students answering exam-type questions. What you do is tell your students to use the question as a statement with

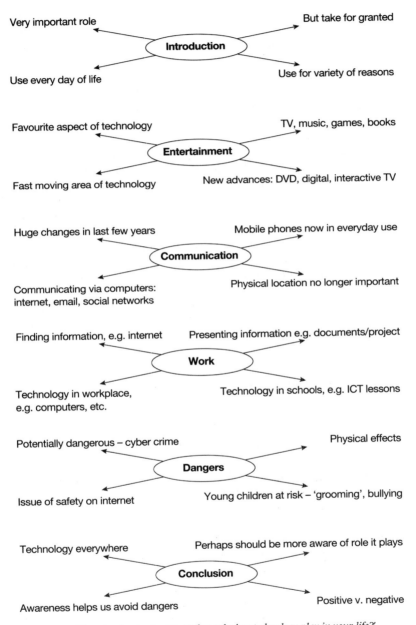

Figure 6.1 Planning brainstorms: *'What role does technology play in your life?'*

which to start their answer. For example, if the question asks them 'In the passage what three things does Fred hate about his school?', they start their answer 'In the passage, Fred hates three things about his school. The first thing that he hates is ...'

✓ *Write out the question*: The physical action of writing out the question at the top of the page gives a strong reminder of the question your students are meant to be answering. In addition, having the question there in front of them will hopefully remind them to stick to it as they write their essay.

✓ *Make a plan*: A well-thought-out plan helps your students structure their essays and stick to the question. The plan is made with the question fresh in the mind, and it helps keep the student 'on track'.

✓ *Keep referring back*: It is easy to become sidetracked when writing a long essay. Encourage your students to re-read the essay question frequently (which is of course written at the top of their answer). Each time she re-reads the question, the student can make a mental check that she is still answering the question. If she is not, she should complete that sentence or paragraph quickly and then get back to the point.

✓ *Be cruel to be kind*: To really make the point, for those students who find it impossible to stick to answer the question, get them to go through their essays with a highlighter. They should highlight *only* those sentences that *directly answer the question*. You can then get them to count up how many sentences they wrote in total, how many related directly to the question, and what percentage of their writing *will actually gain them marks*.

How to quote

Finding and using quotations often causes problems for students, so it's important to teach them the skill of quoting. Share the following ideas and tips with your classes:

✓ *Use short quotes*: Students often feel that they need to use a whole sentence or even a large section of text when quoting. Remind your students that the examiner has access to the text they are discussing. Consequently, they only need to include enough of a quotation to make their point, or to demonstrate to which part of the text they are making reference. A quote of between 5 and 15 words is usually plenty.

✓ *Find the important bit*: Teach your students how to hunt out the most important part of a phrase or sentence for their quote. To give an example, one of the lines from Christina Rossetti's poem 'A birthday' is 'My heart is like a singing bird'. To discuss this simile, a student only needs say 'Rossetti picks the image of "a singing bird" for her simile because …' This sounds less clunky than quoting the whole line, and gives more information – the student knows it's a simile and also that it has been deliberately chosen. When referring to a text (especially one that is reproduced in an exam paper or coursework question), it is safe to assume that the examiner is able to read it too.

✓ *Have a bank of quotes for set texts*: Encourage your students to find a bank of quotes that can be used in exams and coursework essays. These quotes should cover a range of issues (for instance themes, characters, imagery) and be easily accessible (perhaps written in the front of their text, or marked with slips of paper, if this is allowed).

✓ *Don't say 'I quote'*: The use of this phrase jars, and makes the style of an essay sound poor. Encourage them instead to say 'The author says …' or 'The character says …'

The 'four step' essay-writing technique

As both an English teacher and a writer, it occurred to me a number of years ago that it must be possible to offer a technique for writing essays. I wanted to find a strategy that would enable the less skilled to succeed in what can be a very difficult writing task, and also encourage the more able to extend their thinking and their writing. To devise the technique, I took some of my own essays, and broke them down into their constituent parts. What was I doing subconsciously in my writing that made my essays score good marks? And how could I transmit that technique to my students? By answering those questions, I came up with the four-step 'SEED' technique that you'll find described below.

Since I first wrote about this technique, I've come across it in various other places, and in lots of different forms. One particularly amusing form (for older students) was a teacher who had managed to turn the technique into the acronym 'SEX' (Statement, Evidence, Xplain)! Whatever you wish to call your approach, if it works for you and your students, that's all that matters.

The magic of this technique lies in its simplicity: if a student is willing to follow one step with the next in a logical way, she will succeed in writing an essay. This technique has worked for me with weak and poorly motivated students, as well as with borderline C/D GCSE candidates, and also with those working at A/A* standard. It has proved useful when introducing essay writing for the first time with students in lower secondary. It can also be used at a basic level with upper primary aged children, as an early introduction to essay-writing techniques.

The technique involves four steps, each of which provides the student with one or two sentences. Put together, these sentences then create a single paragraph of the essay. The steps are repeated until the essay is finished. I developed this technique for writing English essays, but it is equally applicable to essays in other areas of the curriculum, where essays are required.

The quality of the finished essay will depend on the student's grasp of the ideas or facts they are writing about, on their ability to express themselves and on their higher-order thinking skills. The fourth step ('develop') is the tricky one which differentiates the really able students. The four-step technique helps keep students on-track when answering an essay question. It also gives the less able a chance to write a reasonable essay of their own.

The SEED technique

Imagine a seed being planted in the ground. It is watered, and gradually it grows into a plant, eventually flowering into something beautiful. This is how the 'SEED' technique works – the seed of an idea is planted, the writer cares for it, and it blossoms into a complex, interesting or even beautiful line of thinking.

The four steps are as follows:

1. *Statement*: State something that is true, or make a comment on the subject.
2. *Evidence*: Give evidence or factual detail to support your initial statement.
3. *Explain*: Explain how the evidence links to your initial statement.
4. *Develop*: Develop your ideas, elaborating more fully, or finding a further link.

For weaker students, the fourth step can be left out, and the resulting essay will still be good enough to gain a reasonable grade in an exam or a piece of coursework. Here are two examples of the four-step technique in action. To show that this technique is applicable across much of the curriculum, my examples relate to English Literature and to Science. Now let's consider each step in more detail.

Example 1

1. *Statement*: In *Romeo and Juliet*, Shakespeare makes much use of imagery connected to light.
2. *Evidence*: While Romeo waits below Juliet's balcony, he tells us 'The brightness of her cheek would shame those stars, / As daylight doth a lamp.'
3. *Explain*: Here Romeo uses his words to paint a picture that is saturated with images of light. Just as the daylight is brighter than a lamp, so Romeo feels that Juliet's beauty is so radiant, it would 'shame' even the stars.
4. *Develop*: These images of light contrast strongly with images of darkness, and of the night, particularly at the end of the play, when the lovers die together in a dark tomb.

And here's the full paragraph, as it might appear in an essay:

> In *Romeo and Juliet*, Shakespeare makes much use of imagery connected to light. While Romeo waits below Juliet's balcony, he tells us 'The brightness of her cheek would shame those stars, / As daylight doth a lamp.' Here Romeo uses his words to paint a picture that is saturated with images of light. Just as the daylight is brighter than a lamp, so Romeo feels that Juliet's beauty is so radiant, it would 'shame' even the stars. These images of light contrast strongly with images of darkness, and of the night, particularly at the end of the play, when the lovers die together in a dark tomb.

Example 2

1. *Statement*: Animals with a backbone (vertebrates) are divided into five classes, and these classes of vertebrate are linked by evolution.
2. *Evidence*: The five classes, in order of evolution, are fish, amphibians, reptiles, birds and mammals.
3. *Explain*: The first vertebrates were fish, and from these came the amphibians. The amphibians gave rise to reptiles, which eventually evolved into both birds and mammals.

4. *Develop*: These five classes of vertebrates are divided into cold-blooded creatures (fish, amphibians and reptiles) and warm-blooded animals (birds and mammals).

Again, here's the full paragraph, as it would appear in an essay on this subject:

Animals with a backbone (vertebrates) are divided into five classes, and these classes of vertebrate are linked by evolution. The five classes, in order of evolution, are fish, amphibians, reptiles, birds and mammals. The first vertebrates were fish, and from these came the amphibians. The amphibians gave rise to reptiles, which eventually evolved into both birds and mammals. These five classes of vertebrates are divided into cold blooded (fish, amphibians and reptiles) and warm blooded (birds and mammals).

Writing the statement

Depending on the curriculum area, and on the subject of the essay, the statement might be something that is true (an accepted fact, some factual information, a generally accepted position), or a comment that the student himself believes to be true (an interpretation, a belief). Often, there are subtle degrees of variation between the two. Encourage your students to couch anything they are unsure about as a possibility, supposition or interpretation, rather than stating it as a fact.

Consider these different statements, and whether they are factual, informative, or interpretive:

- The island of Hawaii was formed by volcanic activity under the ocean.
- Wilfred Owen is generally regarded as one of the finest of the war poets writing during the First World War.
- Owen's poem 'Dulce et decorum est' deals with the futility of war – in the poem he questions whether it really is noble to die in battle for your country.
- In Shakespeare's *Twelfth Night* the use of disguise to hide a character's real gender leads to much comedy and confusion.
- In my opinion, John Steinbeck was one of the greatest writers of the twentieth century.
- To stay healthy, human beings need to eat a diet that includes certain vitamins and minerals.

Finding the evidence

The evidence to support the statement can take different forms. Encourage your students to experiment with using different approaches:

✓ *Factual detail*: In some subjects and topics there are factual details for students to use. These facts stretch across the curriculum and include scientific and geographic discoveries and data, accepted terminology, and details such as a person's date of birth or when one country invaded another.

✓ *Quotation*: Quotes may take the form of a line, phrase or sentence from a text that illustrates the statement. They might also be a quote from a textbook in which the author makes a statement that supports the initial contention.

✓ *Events*: Your students might describe an event to support their statement. For instance, in an English essay they might use something that happens in the plot to illustrate a character's personality or an important theme in the story. Alternatively, in a history essay, the event described could be an actual historical incident related to the original statement.

Let's take a couple of the statements above, and show the kind of evidence that might be used to support them:

- *Statement*: In Shakespeare's *Twelfth Night* the use of disguise to hide a character's real gender leads to much comedy and confusion.
- *Evidence*: When Viola dresses as a boy, and goes to work for the Count Orsino, little does she realize that he will fall in love with 'him'.
- *Statement*: To stay healthy, human beings need to eat a diet that includes certain vitamins and minerals.
- *Evidence*: Two of the most important vitamins for health are Vitamin C and Vitamin D.

Explaining the link

The third step involves exploring the link between the initial statement and the evidence that has been given. The ability to make these links between comment, and evidence for that comment, is one of the most important skills in essay writing. Exploring or explaining the link forces the student to ensure that the initial statement has been well thought-out, and that the evidence given does actually support the statement that has been made. The statement is developed, enhanced and extended.

Exploring the link might be a simple explanation of how the quote or evidence does actually support the statement that has been made. For instance, in the example from *Romeo and Juliet* above, the writer notes that the picture Romeo paints with his words is 'saturated with light'. Explaining the link can also involve a development of both the statement and the evidence: in the same example, the writer goes on to explain exactly how the light-based image itself actually works.

Note: in the first example below, you'll see how each step does not necessarily have to be a single sentence – here, a second point in explanation seems merited.

- *Statement*: In Shakespeare's *Twelfth Night* the use of disguise to hide a character's real gender leads to much comedy and confusion.
- *Evidence*: When Viola dresses as a boy, and goes to work for the Count Orsino, little does she realize that they will fall in love with each other.
- *Explain*: Because Orsino believes that Viola is a boy, he is confused by his feelings and tries hard not to acknowledge them. Similarly, Viola cannot reveal the truth of her feelings for him.
- *Statement*: To stay healthy, human beings need to eat a diet that includes certain vitamins and minerals.
- *Evidence*: Two of the most important vitamins for human health are Vitamin C and Vitamin D.
- *Explain*: Vitamin C helps human beings ward off infection, whilst Vitamin D is vital for healthy skin and strong bones.

Developing the point

The fourth step – development – is typically the hardest for students to grasp. However, the first three steps will still provide them with the bare bones of a reasonable essay. The fourth step is the difference between a student who might achieve a grade D–F at GCSE, and a student who is capable of a achieving a grade A–C. Or to put it a better way, between a student who is a good writer, and one who shows flashes of greatness.

Development of a point can take place in one of the following ways.

- ✓ *Further explanation*: Development might involve a further indication of ways in which the evidence supports the initial comment.
- ✓ *Links to other areas within the topic or text*: It might also be about finding a link to another area of the subject being explored. For instance, when writing about a fictional text, students might explain how their point relates to other events or significant factors within the text.

✓ *A connection to the social or historical context*: The development could be the student making a connection to the wider context of the subject being discussed. For example, when writing about the theme of the supernatural in *Macbeth*, the point might be developed by discussing the historical context in which the play was written, and the attitudes to witchcraft at this time.

✓ *A lateral connection*: The development could also be the student making a lateral connection to another idea or area within the topic. This could mean a student writing about an author's characterization, exploring how the characters in the story might link to influential people in the author's life.

✓ *A wider issue*: Similarly, the development could involve suggesting or explaining a link to a wider issue within the topic. So a student writing about the environment within a science essay might link the points made to the current global environmental situation.

Let's see how this works in practice:

- *Statement*: In Shakespeare's *Twelfth Night* the use of disguise to hide a character's real gender leads to much comedy and confusion.
- *Evidence*: When Viola dresses as a boy, and goes to work for the Count Orsino, little does she realize that they will fall in love with each other.
- *Explain*: Because Orsino believes that Viola is a boy, he is confused by his feelings and he tries hard not to acknowledge them. Similarly, Viola cannot reveal the truth of her feelings for him.
- *Develop*: It is only towards the end of the story, when Viola's true identity is revealed, that they are able to declare their feelings for each other.
- *Statement*: To stay healthy, human beings need to eat a diet that includes certain vitamins and minerals.
- *Evidence*: Two of the most important vitamins for human health are Vitamin C and Vitamin D.
- *Explain*: Vitamin C helps human beings ward off infection, whilst Vitamin D is vital for healthy skin and strong bones.
- *Develop*: Interestingly, Vitamin D can be produced through exposure to the sun, as well as through diet.

Introductions and conclusions

It's surprisingly hard to master the skill of writing introductions and conclusions. Students often find it very hard to get started on an essay, and
end up taking a long time to write only a poor standard of introduction.
A key factor is that the introduction to an extended piece of writing is
often best done after the body of the writing has been finished. This is
fine in a coursework essay, which can be drafted and redrafted, perhaps
on a computer, but it is tricky to do in an examination situation. Planning
brainstorms should help a great deal with this. Another possible approach
for exams is to leave a space before beginning the essay, and to go back
at the end to write the introduction.

The tips below will help your students understand more about the
process of writing introductions and conclusions.

✓ *Give a taste of what is to come*: The best introductions give a flavour of
the essay to come, a general taster of the points that will be made. The
best writers find a way to hint at what is to come, both in the things
that they say and also in the language that they use.
✓ *Use the question to start the essay*: A good way for weaker students to
start an introduction is to turn the question that has been asked into
the opening statement. This is especially helpful for those who have
difficulty getting their essays underway. If the question asks 'What
factors led to the start of the Second World War?' the student could
begin the essay by saying 'There were a number of factors that led to
the outbreak of the Second World War.'
✓ *Use the introduction to introduce the subject*: This point might seem
obvious, but it is often ignored. The aim is to give an introduction to
the writer's viewpoint on the question that has been asked, or to give
a general overview of the topic that is about to be discussed.
✓ *Find a lateral point to make*: In the example given below of an essay
introduction, the point made about the language of movement is
actually relatively peripheral to the overall essay content. However, it
provides an interesting and engaging way into the subject for the
writer and the reader.
✓ *Use the conclusion to summarize the content*: The conclusion should
provide an overall, general summary of what has been discussed in
the essay, summing up the points that have been made. Encourage
your students to come to some sort of actual conclusion, especially if
the essay question has asked for specific comment on a topic. For

instance, in answer to a question asking 'Which of these two characters do you most sympathize with?', the student should include a summary of the opinions they have given and come to a definitive answer to the question asked.

✓ *Don't be afraid of the personal*: In the example below, you will see that the essay ends on a highly personal note. Giving an individual view or comment on a subject can be a strong way of concluding an essay, especially one that is about a subject of importance to the writer.

✓ *Don't be afraid of the emotional*: Similarly, if it is relevant to the subject under discussion (for instance in an interpretive piece of writing, or one that analyses a fictional text), a strong conclusion will often involve the declaration of an emotional response to the subject of the essay.

✓ *Avoid direct reference to the content*: When unsure of what to write, students sometimes make the introduction a list of what will be in the essay, and the conclusion a list of what has just been said. This will read in a very pedestrian style, and will not gain them any marks. Where it is applicable to tell the reader what you're about to write, this list should come in the second paragraph of the essay ('In this essay I will be exploring ...').

Perhaps the best way to illustrate the points above is to look at an example of an introduction and a conclusion. These are based around the topic of dance – many years ago, before becoming a teacher/author, I trained as a professional dancer, and therefore this topic is very close to my heart!

Essay question

Discuss the role that dance should play within schools, considering its strengths and weaknesses as part of an increasingly crowded curriculum. What problems must be solved if dance is to play a full and valuable role in the educational experience?

Introduction

People use the language of movement when an experience touches them deeply – we might say 'I am walking on air' or 'my heart leapt'. These instinctive metaphors give us an insight into the fundamental role that movement plays in our lives. It is understandable that teachers neglect dance and movement: burdened with a heavy workload and a lack of experience in this area, there are other issues that probably seem more pressing. However, I feel it is vital to challenge the attitude that sport alone is adequate to satisfy our children's physical needs. There are so many educational possibilities inherent within movement lessons – dance helps us to develop not only our physical skills, but also our imaginative and creative abilities.

Conclusion

Dance has been a part of my life for 20 years. The expression and insight that it has given me have been instrumental in the development of my character. Dance allows us to express ourselves imaginatively and creatively. It also provides a wonderful opportunity for physical activity. If teachers can provide opportunities for their children to experience the richness inherent in movement and dance activities, I believe they will find its value and importance priceless in their students' education.

7

Creative Writing

I saw the angel in the marble and carved until I set him free.

Michelangelo

Creative writing can – and should – happen right across the school curriculum. Although stories, scripts and poems are traditionally forms used within an English or literacy lesson, they actually provide a useful way into writing in many different subjects. Creative writing appeals strongly to children and young people – they welcome the chance to use their imagination, to invent characters or create storylines of their own. The students we teach are surrounded by creative writing outside school, through the whole range of the media – television, computer games, comics, magazines and songs.

Creative writing offers an outlet for your students to express themselves, to make their own mark, to harness the power of their imagination. While the students you teach might not have the potential to be a Dickens, a Shakespeare or a Michelangelo (although perhaps one of them might!), each and every one of them has something unique and imaginative of their own to express through the written word. In this chapter you will find lots of ideas, tips and advice about helping your students develop the myriad skills and techniques involved in creative writing.

Creating a fiction

As teachers, we spend much of our time creating 'fictions' for our students. A teacher who uses the 'strict and scary' model described in my book *Getting the Buggers to Behave* (4th edition, Continuum, 2010), is creating a fiction about herself. Few of us are strict and scary people in our lives outside school. A teacher who uses this model in her professional life wouldn't shout at or be scary with her friends and family. However, she finds that by creating this fiction about herself within school she gets better behaviour from her students.

115

Our students, too, are complicit in the fictions we create: schools are reliant on the students' willingness to go along with these fictions to maintain a sense of order and control. There is no real reason why the class should behave for and obey their teacher, but, in the majority of cases, they do. Students love being part of a fiction; as teachers we should utilize this to engage with them and motivate them in their writing.

Starting points for creative writing

In this first section of the chapter, you'll find lots of useful starting points for creative writing. You'll find ideas here for quick starter activities, inspiring your class, playing with genre, and lots more.

Starter activities

Use these quick, focused activities as warm-ups for fictional writing, as ways to focus your students, or just to get them thinking:

✓ *The 20 word story*: The students are going to write a story, but it must be exactly 20 words long. Not 19, not 21, but exactly 20. Give a short time limit, about two or three minutes, to do it, then listen to the results.
✓ *The 'no E' story*: Again, the students write a short story, but this time it must not include any words that contain the letter 'e'. It's trickier than it sounds.
✓ *The five-word sentence story*: Along the same lines, the students write a short piece in which each sentence contains exactly five words.
✓ *Last lines*: Read the last few lines or paragraph of a story book. Working in pairs, your students tell each other the rest of the story.

Finding inspiration

Finding inspiration for writing might be about discovering the initial spark for a story or poem, or about choosing ways to develop a piece of descriptive writing more fully. Inspiration comes in many shapes and forms: here are some suggestions to help you find it:

✓ *Props*: Students love having an item to work with, especially something that is out of place in the classroom. Working with a prop might lead to ideas for a character, a place, an event. Have a large box of different props in your classroom to help whenever inspiration is needed – include different bags and purses, some jewellery boxes, feathers, stones, shells, money from different countries, playing cards, photos, and so on.

✓ *Associations*: Find inspiration by making associations between one thing and another: for instance, between an exotic piece of fruit and the place it came from. Smell is a particularly strong sense when it comes to forming associations. Discuss links between a smell/sound and a place – what do they associate with a hospital, a shopping centre, a zoo, an airport?

✓ *Bag of words*: Have a bag of words for your children to dip into – include unusual words, ones that stimulate the imagination. Alternatively, display your words on a board with Velcro, and allow students to pick words to inspire their writing.

✓ *Music*: Listen to music to inspire your students' imagination, and make them think of different moods, places, people, etc. Start the lesson by listening to music, to help your students get focused.

Using your senses

Most of us naturally use our sight and hearing when we are writing creatively, but of course we can also explore taste, touch and smell. Here are some ideas to get your students using their senses more fully in their written work.

✓ *Senses brainstorm*: This approach is useful before writing a poem or story and it can also be used for other areas of the curriculum. Ask your students to brainstorm vocabulary under the headings of see, hear, taste, touch and smell.

✓ *Remove one sense*: Deprive your students of one of their senses to encourage them to use their other senses more fully. Remove the sense of sight with a blindfold, then give a variety of objects for your students to touch, smell, listen to and taste. Remove the sense of touch, by asking your students to put their hands behind their back, and then to describe how different objects would feel without touching them.

✓ *Colours*: This is a fun exercise that I did when I was at school (and have remembered ever since, which proves it was engaging). You may be sceptical about it, but give it a try. It provides an excellent way into writing about colours, and creates a strong sense of focus. Blindfold a volunteer and put a sheet of coloured paper in front of him. Ask him to touch the paper and focus very hard on 'feeling' the colour. Some students have a much higher 'hit rate' than others.

✓ *Weather*: Ask your students to shut their eyes and imagine a type of weather (you specify this), for instance a storm. Now ask them to move through their senses, one at a time, as you say them. What can they see? What can they hear? What can they feel, and so on. This can lead to some excellent descriptive writing. It also encourages students to empathize with their characters, feeling what a character might feel if she was stuck outside during a storm, or trapped on a desert island in the heat.

Sound tracking

I love this activity for the way that it requires the students to work together as a single unit. It is a fabulous way to get them thinking about the senses, and about how to create atmosphere. The idea is to create a place or setting, using sound.

✓ Get your students to lie in a circle on the floor, with their feet facing out of the circle and their heads nearly touching. (This gives the best possible effect sound-wise).

✓ Specify a setting for them to create, for instance a prison leading up to a riot, a ship in a storm, a haunted house on a windy night, a Victorian asylum, and so on.

✓ They are going to create this setting *using only sound*. They might make sounds with their mouths, but they can also use their bodies as appropriate.

✓ They should start quietly, adding sounds as and when they feel it is appropriate. Not everyone has to make a sound at once.

✓ Get your class to build the sound effects up to a climax, before ending, either by fading out, or by stopping abruptly.

✓ When it's going well, the class should be able to make a group judgement (without the need for any kind of signal) as to when is a good point to fade out or stop the soundtrack.

You may find at first that your students are too noisy, or that they do not work well together. However, with practice, you will find that the 'places' created can be extraordinarily powerful and inspirational. Record the exercise, either to play back to your children, or to use as a 'mood' tape for writing.

The importance of genre

One of the best ways into any piece of writing for the teacher is via genre, and this applies especially to creative writing. Genre is a French word which literally translates as 'type'. The children of the twenty-first century are positively steeped in genre: through the movies they watch, the books they read, the television programmes they see and the computer games they play. Certain genres really capture the children's attention, for instance science fiction, crime, horror. The *Harry Potter* phenomenon has seen an upsurge of interest in magic and fantasy, both in books and onscreen. By approaching creative writing via genre, we can spark our students' interest and get them motivated in their work.

The elements of genre

Asking our students to write within a genre gives us a wonderful chance to exercise their writing skills. They must select the correct elements to include: the right types of character, the likely locations, the appropriate words and terminology. They must also think carefully about audience expectations when writing within a specific genre. Generally speaking, genres follow set rules, though many of the best genre stories either break or subvert these rules in some way. A story in the magic genre is almost honour-bound to feature witches and wizards, while a story in the crime genre is going to feature a criminal, a victim and a detective at the very least. The typical elements of genre include:

- characters
- location
- storyline
- 'lighting' and atmosphere
- 'props' (objects)
- costume or clothing
- type of dialogue
- likely vocabulary
- plot events or features.

Pick a genre, and ask your students to list the 'standard elements' that they would expect to find. For instance, in a crime story, you might have the following features:

- characters: victim, criminal, 'scapegoat', witnesses, detective, police officers
- location: back alley, police station, bank, getaway car
- storyline: a crime takes place; the police work to solve it; the criminal is caught
- 'lighting' and atmosphere: dark, foggy streets; tense, scary atmosphere
- 'props': weapons, handcuffs, evidence, photofit posters
- costume or clothing: police uniforms, a bloodstained shirt, prison uniforms
- type of dialogue: formal language used by police, criminal might use slang
- likely vocabulary: crime, criminal, victim, witness, forensics, fingerprints, etc.
- plot events or features: the discovery of a body, the clue that is a 'red herring'.

Study a selection of texts from different genres to identify the various elements that define the genre of each piece. Get your students writing in different genres, using the ideas given below for inspiration.

Setting an atmosphere for genre writing

The use of genres offers you a wonderful opportunity to create an atmosphere or mood in your classroom. By doing this, you spark your students' interest, and engage their attention, inspiring them when they come to actually write. To create an atmosphere for genre writing in your classroom, you might use:

✓ lighting effects – a blackout, candles, torches
✓ sound effects – animal noises, weather sounds
✓ objects – props and other items related to the genre
✓ costumes – for the teacher/students to wear
✓ in-role work – with the teacher/students taking on characters from the genre.

Playing with genre

Playing around with genre is a very useful and highly motivating approach to creative writing. For example, you might start by asking your class to rewrite various genre extracts into another genre. Students seem to love subverting or adapting the original form and intentions of a piece of writing. When they do this, they are learning about and developing an understanding of the conventions of different written forms.

I experienced a wonderful example of the way that forms and genres can be played with or subverted when I was teaching my very first Year 9 class in preparation for their external SAT tests. We had studied *Romeo and Juliet* in some detail, and we were working on the party scene, where the young lovers meet for the first time. We had also been exploring slang and dialect, discussing the language that Shakespeare used, and how his plays might sound today. I set an activity to translate the party scene into modern-day language, adding slang or using dialect as the class wished. Two of my students, who came from an Afro-Caribbean background, worked together to produce a fantastic patois version of the scene, which we performed in class.

Here is an extract from their scene, showing the impressive way in which they were able to play with the original words and subvert the form in a way that perhaps Shakespeare himself might well have enjoyed!

Rochon and JuJu
[Enter MASTER CARLTON, MISS CAROL, JUJU, TYRONE, 'ELPER and guests.]

CARLTON: Welcome ladies and gentlemen. Which one of you lovely ladies want fi dance? If you say no a corns you a grow pon dem foot, come bus' out the tune, nam and drink until your belly bus!

[Ladies kiss their teef and look away.]

Come rest yourself cos.
CARLOS: Jesus peace a thirty years since mi last see you.
CARLTON: A nuh that long. It was at Lucil wedding.
CARLOS: Oh yes, mi remember that well. That was in the old days when we were young and lively.
CARLTON: Those were the days man!
ROCHON: Who's that pretty woman over deh so?
SERVANT 1: Mi nuh know sir.
ROCHON: She kinda nice you know. We warn fi teck her to mi yard tonight. Mi just go teck a little breeze over deh so.

Here are some more ideas for subverting and playing with genre in your classroom:

✓ *Subvert audience expectations*: When we read a story, we do so with certain expectations about what will happen and how the characters will behave within that genre. This is especially so with the genre of fairy tales: these stories have simple, traditional plots, and use highly stereotyped characters. By subverting audience expectations, writers can create some wonderful and humorous effects. For instance, the author Babette Cole confounds audience expectations by rewriting Cinderella as 'Prince Cinders'.

✓ *Change the form*: Changing the form in which a story is presented produces interesting and often hilarious results. For instance, your students might rewrite and perform the story of *The Three Little Pigs*:
  – as a football match report
  – as a TV new story
  – as a 'Jerry Springer'-style chat show (*Wolfie's Story*)
  – as an opera
  – as a soap opera
  – as a tabloid-style 'celebrity' magazine.

✓ *Update and change the language*: In the *Romeo and Juliet* example above, although the language has been updated, the meaning of the original has been retained. Your students might write a Victorian melodrama rewritten in the style of *Glee*, or a modern-day crime story in the style of Jane Austen.

✓ *Change the perspective*: Certain genres tend to use specific perspectives. The crime story is often written from the viewpoint of the detective, or the thriller from the perspective of the hero. By shifting the perspective you can achieve some very interesting results. For instance, in the hilarious *Dr Xargle* books, the writers view Earth and Earthlings from the perspective of visiting aliens.

Writing fiction

When writing fiction we work in the realm of the imagination, and our minds can run free. Although writing a story just to learn about writing a story is a task for English lessons, there are many other subject areas where writing fiction is an extremely useful approach to use. Fiction writing gives students a wonderful outlet for their worries and emotions, offering a pretend world in which they can explore those issues they find troubling. For this reason, it can be used to very good effect in a Personal Social Health & economic Education (PSHE) lesson.

The following sections deal with the techniques involved in story writing: much that is covered here will also be applicable to writing scripts.

Creating characters

One of the most exciting things about writing fiction is the chance to create imaginary people (and imaginary creatures too) all of our very own. At first, many young writers tend to write about the people that they know. Constant exposure to television and film may also mean that your young writers fall back on copying plots and characters that they have seen on screen.

Here are lots of ideas for encouraging your students to create interesting and believable characters of their own:

✓ *Props*: Props are an excellent way of developing interesting characters. Bring a piece of clothing into the classroom and ask the children to talk about the different characters who wear it. 'Find' the bag that belongs to a character (perhaps one left at a crime scene), and look at the contents of bag to decide on the type of person who owns it.

✓ *What's in a name*: Give your students some unusual names, and ask them to write about the characters that they visualize. Choose a name that has additional layers of meaning or in which the words hint at the character's personality, such as Cruella de Ville.

✓ *Setting the scene*: Set up a 'scene' in your classroom, which the characters have just left. To give an example that I have used myself, you might put:

– two hands of cards on a table
– some coins scattered across the table and onto the floor
– two chairs (one upright, the other overturned)
– an empty glass
– a bottle that has fallen to the floor.

Talk with your students about what has just happened in this scene, and what sort of characters might be in this story. You could ask your students to act out the scene that took place. This type of work can lead to some really inspired story- or scriptwriting.

✓ *Hot seating*: This drama technique is excellent for developing characters, and is loved by students of all ages. It also works well for questioning characters in a text you are studying, whether a GCSE text or a picture book in the primary school.

- Ask for a volunteer to sit in the 'hot seat', facing the rest of the class. This volunteer is going to play a character.
- The character can be invented beforehand, but it is often best to let him or her take shape as you go along.
- You can do this by asking questions that force the person in the 'hot seat' to invent the story of this character on the spot.
- For instance, the teacher begins by saying 'I understand that you were seen running away from the Royal Oak public house, covered in blood? Can you tell me what you had to do with the murder of Fred Bloggs?'
- The character in the 'hot seat' responds to this and the questions that follow.

✓ *The 'judgement chair'*: This is another drama technique that will help your students invent rounded and interesting characters. Again, it can be used for questioning characters who already exist in a text you are studying, or for developing new ones. It can also be used to study citizenship topics or PSHE issues such as teenage pregnancy or drug abuse.
- A volunteer sits in the 'judgement chair'.
- Various other characters from that person's life come up to pass judgement on her.
- The volunteer may respond in role to the judgements, or she might simply listen to what is said.
- For instance, you might use the scenario of a child who has been caught shoplifting.
- The characters judging the child could include her parents, brothers and sisters, police officers and teachers.
- The parents might come up to her and say 'How could you do this to us? We're so disappointed in you.'

✓ *What do I need to know?* To give depth to their fictional characters, encourage your students to invent lots of background information for the people they make up. Not all this information will be included in the creative writing, but it helps the writer create a more realistic character. This is known as a character's 'back story' in fiction-writing circles. The information could come under various categories, for instance physical, social, psychological, emotional. Some of the things they might need to know include:
- what the character looks like
- what he wears
- who his parents are
- what his childhood was like

- what job he does
- what makes him angry
- what makes him happy
- what he likes to spend his money on.

Your students could create a fact sheet for their character, or they could script an interview, with a partner asking the questions.

Show, don't tell

A classic mistake that many young (and indeed old) writers make in their fiction is to *tell* the reader what is happening, rather than *show* them. This is how young children first write their stories: 'Anna was sad. She was sad because she lost her teddy', and so on. This 'listing' technique is also prevalent in essays – the student 'lists' all the facts she knows about a subject, without developing any of the ideas further, or relating them to the question.

It's important to 'show' rather than 'tell' because it helps to:

✓ *Maintain the illusion*: The ideal in our writing is for there to be nothing that intrudes between the reader and what he is reading, nothing that 'breaks the spell' of the text. When the writer *tells* the reader what is happening in her story, this creates an authorial intrusion that lessens the strength of the text. Instead of allowing the reader to work things out for himself, the writer feels the need to explain what her characters are thinking and feeling. A writer who is 'telling' might say 'Shami was really angry'. A writer who is 'showing' might say 'Shami clenched her fists and a dark look came over her face.'

✓ *Encourage empathy*: Showing invites the reader to step into the character's shoes, to empathize totally with them, even psychologically 'becoming' that person while he or she is reading. It is this empathy that we are talking about when we say we became 'lost' in a book: it was so engrossing we forgot all about the real world.

✓ *Treat the reader right*: By showing rather than telling, the writer makes an assumption about his or her readers – that they are intelligent and interested enough to work out the characters' emotions for themselves, rather than needing to be held by the hand and told.

✓ *Maintain the quality of the writing*: Showing encourages a more visual, detailed writing style, because the writer is forced to describe the characters and what they do in detail, rather than using blunt phrases such as 'she was sad/angry/happy'. It also tends to create a style with more energy and pace, rather than a series of plodding 'facts', as you will see in the examples given below.

✓ *Maintain the quality of the characterization*: Similarly, the writer has to create more realistic, believable characters: how would this character behave if she were angry, what mannerisms or actions might she use?

If you think about the way in which the best stories work, it is because the reader can visualise the people and events in his imagination. You see the story happening before your eyes, and this allows you to empathize with the characters, drawing you into the story. You have no need for the author to tell you what the characters are thinking and feeling – you know already, because you 'see' them in your head. The following examples demonstrate the difference between 'telling' and 'showing' the reader.

Example 1: 'Telling' the reader

Julie was very sad. She knew that she didn't have any friends. This made her feel terrible, and she hated going to school each day. She knew that Katie and Emma hated her most of all. She felt like hitting Emma. It was all Emma's fault. But she didn't know what to do about it.

Example 2: 'Showing' the reader

A tear trickled down Julie's cheek. 'I'm not going to school,' she told her mum.

'Oh yes you are,' her mum replied.

A bitter knot of resentment pulled at Julie's stomach as she tugged on her school uniform. Dashing the tears from her cheeks, she thought back to what had happened in the playground the day before.

'You're not playing with us,' Katie said. Emma was standing behind her, a twisted smile on her face.

Julie clenched her fists hard, her fingernails biting into her palms, her head swimming with thoughts of revenge.

Narrative voice and viewpoint

Before writing a story, it is essential for the writer to establish where he stands in relation to his characters and his readers. There are three 'basic' narrative voices, of which the two most commonly used are explained below. With the third option, the 'omniscient viewpoint', the writer assumes a 'godlike' position, overseeing everything that happens in the story. This viewpoint can feel quite intrusive, and tends not to appeal to modern readers. The 'second person' viewpoint is rarely used any more in fiction.

✓ *First-person viewpoint*: The story is told from the perspective of the first person, using 'I' as the narrative voice. The person speaking might be one of the characters in the story, or it could be the voice of the writer. This narrative voice encourages the reader to associate strongly with the character telling the story, as we see events from her perspective. However, the writer cannot include events that his narrator does not experience directly.

✓ *Third-person viewpoint*: The story is told from a third person perspective, using 'she' or 'he'. Stories using a third-person narrator are usually told mainly from the viewpoint of one character, with the writer allowing us access to the thoughts and feelings of this one person. Sometimes, however, two or more characters may be used. This viewpoint does not create such a strong sense of empathy, as the reader is not viewing the story through the eyes of one person. However, the writer can describe events outside the direct experience of his or her characters.

Dialogue

We might think that writing dialogue should be the easiest thing in the world. After all, we spend our lives communicating through speech. Surely all we need to do is turn our spoken words into written ones? However, there is much more to writing interesting and exciting dialogue than simply transferring speech onto the page. Here are some tips about how you can encourage your students to write imaginative and effective speech for the characters in their stories. Many of these ideas will also apply to the process of writing play-scripts.

✓ *Conflict, conflict, conflict*: Conflict is a vital aspect in any decent piece of fiction and is a crucial part of writing good dialogue. Having conflicts helps avoid the dreary 'what did you have for breakfast?' type of speech. Some ways that you might help your students inject conflict into their dialogue include the following:

- Conflicting agendas – where one character wants the opposite to the other, and each is fighting for their own position.
- Blocking – where one person is refusing to agree with what the other says, and is throwing up a series of complaints or issues.
- Conflicting personalities – where each character has a very different personality, for instance one person is easily angered, while the other stays calm.

✓ *Avoiding boredom*: Much of what we say in everyday life is entirely lacking in conflict. However, when write a story, we need to find some way of engrossing the reader, otherwise she will stop reading. One useful way of avoiding boredom is to twist what might have been a normal conversation into something a little more exciting, for instance by including details specific to the characters involved. In the examples below you will see how a mundane conversation about the time has been turned into something altogether more interesting.

✓ *Twisting the words*: What we say and what we mean can be two very different things. There is often a subtext going on behind our words, and this makes things more interesting for the reader. Encourage your students to play with dialogue and meaning, to have their characters saying one thing while meaning something else, or misinterpreting what the other person says. Try this 'devil on my shoulder' exercise to get your students thinking about this idea:
- Split the class into groups of four.
- Two of them are going to have what seems to be a fairly normal conversation on the surface; two of them are going to play the 'devil on my shoulder'.
- This means that they are going to say the subtext of the conversation out loud.
- For instance, the first person says 'Hello Anna, love your new haircut.'
- The 'devil' says: 'NOT! Are you planning to sue your hairdresser?'

✓ *Learning to listen*: Encourage your students to listen to the speech that surrounds them, for instance the conversations that they might overhear on the school bus in the morning. Set a homework task, asking them to make a note of three unusual or interesting lines of dialogue that they overhear during the course of a day, and building a story around them.

✓ *Thinking about character*: The way that we speak tells other people a lot about our personality, upbringing and background. For instance, an elderly gentleman who spent his life in the army would use speech very differently to a young child on her first day at school.

✓ *Communicating tone*: The tone of characters' voices can be communicated in a variety of ways. It's most tempting for your students to use a range of verbs and adverbs, such as 'he shouted' or 'he said angrily'. However, these dialogue 'tags' become very intrusive for the reader, especially if a number of them are used within one section of dialogue. A better option is to try to make the words themselves and the way that they are structured hint at the tone of a character's voice.

✓ *The invisible 'said'*: The word 'said' is, to a large extent, 'invisible' to the reader, and it allows them to focus instead on the dialogue itself. It is often a much better option than more visually intrusive words such as 'answered' or 'replied'.

✓ *Removing the dialogue tags*: It is often possible to actually remove dialogue tags such as 'said' altogether, particularly if there are only two characters speaking in a scene. Once it has been established who is speaking and in what order, there is no real need for any further explanation.

Example 1: How not to write dialogue

'What time is it?' Jamie asked breathlessly.

'Half past two,' Tara answered calmly.

'It's nearly time to go back to work then,' Jamie said with a sigh.

'Do we have to?' Tara moaned plaintively.

'Yes,' Jamie answered with finality.

Example 2: How to write dialogue

Jamie glanced at his bare wrist. 'Tara, you got the time?'

'The time for what?' She winked at him and flashed a smile.

'No, what time is it?' He tapped his wrist to indicate where a watch should have been. Tara's smile vanished.

'How the hell should I know the time, Jamie? What happened to that watch I gave you for your birthday?'

'It's ...'

'Don't tell me you've broken it already, Jamie.'

'Don't start, Tara.'

'What do you mean, "don't start"? That watch cost me a bloody fortune.'

'Why is everything about money with you, Tara?'

Setting

The great thing about fiction is that it can take place in any setting that your students choose, from the mountains of Borneo to the snowy wastes of Alaska, from the streets of London to a spaceship on a mission to Mars. Writers are often encouraged to 'write about what you know'. Although our students might not have had much opportunity to travel abroad, most of them will have had ample opportunity to see other places and lives on the television. In many cases, it's best for them simply to use their imagination.

When you are setting up your classroom for some creative writing, you could turn one part or even your whole room into 'another place', to inspire your students. You might:

✓ set up a haunted house by blacking out your room and adding some spooky sound effects
✓ for a story about Native American Indians, get your class to work as a 'tribe', inventing their own tribal name and rituals, and having 'pow-wows' sitting in a circle on the floor
✓ line up the chairs to make airplane seats, and then fly off somewhere exotic
✓ put a 'magic carpet' on the floor, to inspire journeys to imaginary magical and fantastical places.

The importance of conflict

A story without conflict is boring. If the character does not face any problems or difficulties in his fictional journey, the reader has no reason to become involved in the story. Conflict adds tension for the reader. We become caught up in the story because we are worried for the characters, fearful that they might be in danger of some kind. Adding conflict to a story makes the difference between a dull piece of writing and an interesting one. A writer who does not use conflict might tell a story where Fred gets up in the morning, goes to school, comes home, does his homework and goes to bed. A writer who uses conflict might have Fred getting up in the morning and overhearing his parents having a huge quarrel, or have Fred arrive at school to find that aliens have taken over his world, and he is the only one who realizes. At once, the reader is engaged and wants an answer to the question 'what happens next?'

Learning to include conflict in stories is one of the fundamental lessons of good fiction writing which your students must learn. There are three basic conflicts: person against person, person against nature, and person against him- or herself. Here are some ideas for different ways of getting your students to introduce conflict, and consequently tension, into their stories:

✓ *Problems*: Readers instinctively engage with a character who is experiencing problems, because they want to know what is going to happen, and whether the character will overcome the challenge. The more problems that your students throw at their characters, the higher the level of conflict and tension will rise. These problems might be:
   – a character who has trouble making friends
   – someone with a medical problem that must be overcome
   – a person who is experiencing financial problems
   – a character who faces an ethical dilemma
   – an external, physical problem, for instance a character who gets lost in a storm.

✓ *Obstacles:* When an obstacle stands between a character and his or her goal, this creates conflict. (For instance, in the classic example of *Romeo and Juliet*, the obstacle that the two lovers face is the hatred between the two families.) It is important that the goal is clear – that the reader realizes what the character is striving for, and how the obstacles are preventing her from reaching her goal.

✓ *Between characters*: Conflict also arises between the hero/heroine and the villain in a story. This conflict might be apparent in the actions that they take, for instance fighting with each other, or in the dialogue between them.

Here are some specific exercises to use in your classroom when teaching your students about conflict.

✓ *The worst thing*: Decide on a character with your class, for instance a boy who loves to play football, or a dog who is terrified of storms. Now ask them to think of some of the worst things that could happen to that character. For the boy who loves football, it could be breaking his leg, or being given a detention that means he misses a crucial match. For the scared dog, it could be that her owners shut her outside during a storm, or that she must go out into the storm to save someone. Immediately, these scenarios offer your students conflict with which to make their stories exciting.

✓ *You can't have it because* ...: Conflict is created when a character is prevented from having what he or she wants. Ask your students to think of a character who really, really wants something: for instance a girl

131

who desperately wants to go out with a boy in her class, or an astronaut who desperately wants to fly to the moon. Ask for volunteers to come to the front of the classroom and tell the class 'What I want most in the whole world is ...' Then the rest of the class must come up with all the reasons they can't have it. As they suggest these reasons, the volunteer can come up with ideas for overcoming the obstacles, to include in a story.

✓ *A series of problems*: As we saw above, a single problem will cause conflict, but a series of problems (preferably rising in difficulty and danger as they progress) will cause an ever-increasing level of tension. To experiment with this, give your students a scenario (for instance, a group of children who go out for a trip on a boat), and ask them to come up with a series of problems for the characters to encounter, of increasing danger and complexity. For instance, in the scenario given, their series of problems might run as follows:
  - One of the children feels seasick.
  - The map falls overboard and they get lost.
  - A storm starts to brew.
  - The boat springs a leak.
  - They find that there is a hole in the lifeboat.
  - The boat starts to sink.
  - The storm begins to rage.
  - The boat sinks and the children are thrown in the water.
  - The sharks arrive!

The importance of dramatic tension

Dramatic tension is closely linked to conflict. Dramatic tension is what keeps the reader (or audience) 'on the edge of their seat'. It is what involves us with a story and its characters, and makes us want to read on to find out what happens. Your students can develop dramatic tension through the use of conflict, as described above. However, there are lots of other ways for them to produce dramatic tension as well:

✓ *Vocabulary*: The type of words used when writing a story can be very effective in creating and developing dramatic tension, especially within certain genres. For instance, in a ghost story words such as 'creak', 'howl', 'terror' and 'petrified' would all help to keep the reader feeling tense and nervous.

✓ *Sentence structure*: The length and structure of sentences can also add to the level of tension created, and it is worthwhile studying examples from the thriller or action genres to see how this works. Writers will use a series of very short sentences to create a feeling of breathy, nervous tension.

✓ *Imagery*: Similes, metaphors and other images can be used to great effect when adding tension to a story. The images that a writer employs may hint at danger below the surface, as in the example below, where the gargoyles have 'faces like demons', clearly suggesting that evil is in the air.

✓ *Lighting and 'special effects'*: The best stories often have a cinematic feel to them, and when we think about films that are full of tension, there is often much use made of lighting and other special effects. It could be that darkness is used to hide the danger that lurks all around, or that a mist suddenly descends on a group of children as they walk through the forest.

✓ *Sound effects*: Similarly, in scary or tense films, sounds will often be used to add to the tension. In the example below, notice how the sound that Danny hears adds to the frightening atmosphere.

✓ *Character responses*: The way that a character responds to a situation will also help create tension. The reader senses the fear that the character is feeling, for instance when Danny shivers in the example below, this heightens the feeling that danger is close by.

✓ *The 'cliffhanger'*: A cliffhanger is often found at the end of chapters in novels, but can also be used in shorter stories. The cliffhanger simply leaves the reader 'hanging' in the air, wondering 'what did happen next?' Sometimes their question is answered, sometimes the writer jumps to a later point in the story, leaving the reader's question unresolved for the time being.

✓ *Enclosed spaces*: Tension is often at its highest when we are confined or restricted in some way. For instance, if a lift gets stuck between floors there is the opportunity for tension to arise (especially if one of the characters in the lift is claustrophobic, or has some other sort of pressing problem).

✓ *Story questions*: A story question occurs when the reader notices something within the story that seems to be significant. Within the reader's mind, he or she thinks 'Aha! I spotted something important!', and this increases the sense of involvement for the reader. For instance, the writer might mention in passing an object that later turns out to be a clue to the murderer's identity. In the example below, we hear of 'that case in '92', which is mentioned only in passing, but which is clearly going to be significant in the story.

The following example shows how some of these ideas work together to create a high level of tension. I have used the supernatural genre, as this naturally lends itself to a feeling of fear and danger. You can download a copy of this text, to use with your class, at the companion website.

> Danny looked up at the dark stone castle, just visible in the deepening gloom. Gargoyles hung from the battlements, their faces like demons, watching him, laughing at him. A cold wind swept down from the distant mountains and made him shiver. He pulled his coat tighter and tried to stop shaking. They had dared him to do this. To go inside. Inside the Castle of Terror. That was what they had called it. He laughed at them when they said that.
>
> 'Don't believe in the supernatural then, Dan?' Johnny asked.
>
> Dan laughed again. 'Nah, it's rubbish,' he answered, but with a rising sense of dread.
>
> 'Dare yeh to spend the night in there, then,' Johnny challenged him.
>
> Well, he could not turn back now. He had no choice. And besides, he didn't believe in the supernatural. It was all a load of rubbish.
>
> Suddenly there was a hideous sound, half scream, half moan. Danny span around. The sound had come from behind him. From the forest. Out of the blackness. He could make out something moving towards him through the mist. He turned back to the building. What should he do? Go into the Castle of Terror? Stay out here? 'It's just Johnny trying to scare me,' he told himself. But as he turned back to the creature, and saw what it was, a scream escaped from his mouth. It was the last sound he ever made.
>
> 'We got us a body here, Jim,' the policeman spoke into his radio. 'Looks like some maniac on the loose. Bad injuries, ain't seen nothing this nasty in a long long time. Not since, you know, that case in '92. You better get the forensics team out here right away.'

Dramatic irony

Finally, a technique called dramatic irony can also be put to very good use by your students when injecting conflict into their creative writing. This complicated-sounding term is actually quite simple to understand. Dramatic irony describes a situation in which the reader (or audience, with a play) knows something that one or more of the characters do not. For instance, in a novel the reader knows that the murderer is hiding in the heroine's bedroom. As the heroine climbs up the stairs to bed, tension is created by the reader's urge to warn her about the danger that lies in wait.

Writing scripts

There are a number of important differences between writing a script and writing a story, and it is important for students to understand this before they attempt to write scenes or plays of their own. When they first write a script, many children will use a narrator to describe the events that are taking place. Rather than this being a deliberate choice, it tends to be because they are inexperienced in telling a story through dialogue. Resorting to a narrator means that they can put across the action by telling the audience what is happening, rather than showing them this through what the characters say and do.

The section in this chapter on dialogue gives you some ideas about writing effective speech, and these apply just as readily to scripts as to stories or novels. When writing scripts, take the time to talk to your students about exactly what makes this particular form of writing special. Here are some ideas that you might like to consider, including advice on some of the more common pitfalls that students experience.

✓ *Audience*: A script is written to be performed, rather than read. Scripts are aimed at a 'live' audience (whether in a theatre, or watching a television show or film), rather than a reader sitting with a book. When writing scripts, encourage your students to visualize their scripts being performed, rather than viewing them as static dialogue on the page. Some of the best scripts come out of practical work – improvisations in which the storyline and characters gradually appear, and which are then put down on paper.

✓ *Characters*: In a script, we learn about the characters through the things that they say and do, and the way that they appear. This means that the dialogue must work hard to show us what these people are like. The writer might also include stage directions to show the director or actors how the lines should be spoken, how the characters should move, and perhaps information about costume to help define character.

✓ *Plot*: The audience can only access the plot through the words and actions of the characters. Many students find it very hard to put across the plot of a story simply through the people involved, and at this point will resort to an onstage narrator to tell the audience what is going on.

✓ *Setting*: Stage directions may be used to explain the location of the events. However, when a play is performed, the setting can only be shown to the audience by set design, furniture, costume and any special effects. Again, the temptation is for your students to use a narrator who gives this information to the audience.

✓ *Special effects*: One of the great things about creating scripts is that it gives your students the chance to be inventive with their use of 'special effects'. Although in reality their play might not be performed, there is no harm in them going to town on the imaginative possibilities, including:
  – lighting – use of colours, bright or dim lights, spotlights, strobe
  – sound – animal sounds, machine sounds, traffic noise
  – other effects – smoke machines, bangs, etc.

Obviously, if you can get your students to perform their scripts, so much the better. I've found it particularly useful to record performances, so that the students can watch them back and analyse what worked well, and what didn't.

✓ *Layout*: Before working on scriptwriting, teach your students the correct layout. They will need to learn elements such as:
  – including a list of characters
  – giving details of the setting
  – how to write speech – character's name, no speech marks, tone of voice in square brackets
  – how to give stage directions – in square brackets
  – use of scenes and acts.

Writing poetry

In my experience, younger students respond well to poetry, and really enjoy writing poems of their own. However, by the time our students get into the later years of secondary school some of them have been 'turned off' the whole idea of poetry as a form for writing. For this reason, as well as talking about general approaches to teaching poetry in this section, I have also included some ideas for teachers who are finding poetry really difficult to teach, whether because of poor class behaviour or lack of interest.

First approaches to poetry

When approaching poetry writing, I would recommend that you start off by digging into exactly what makes a poem a poem. This is surprisingly hard to ascertain. After all, both poetry and prose might include imagery, words that rhyme, rhythmic language, sensory perceptions and so on. At its heart, a poem is a piece of condensed language, one that creates a strong image, a series of word pictures, or a powerful mood. Poetry is also essentially about sound and rhythm, about the way that words sound when they are spoken out loud. However, even these descriptions do not fit all poems.

Here are some questions that you might like to raise with your class:

– What is the difference between a poem and a song?
– If we listen to a song without music, is it a poem?
– Do all poems have to rhyme?
– What is the difference between a non-rhyming poem and a piece of prose?
– How are poems laid out on the page?
– Do all poems tell a story?
– Do all poems have to 'make sense'?
– What makes a good poem?
– Are poems designed to be read on the page, spoken out loud, or both?

Inspirations for poetry

Finding a powerful and engaging inspiration is often the key to success in motivating your students to create their own poetry. The following ideas should give you some ways into writing poems, both for young, emerging writers and for older, more experienced students.

✓ *Events*: When something important or moving happens, writing poetry can be a good way of dealing with our responses. Writing poems provides an excellent way to express our feelings, to turn our emotions into words. For this reason, poetry can be effective when dealing with PSHE issues.

✓ *Places*: Because of its generally descriptive nature, poetry offers an effective format for creating a 'sense of place', a 'word-picture' that captures a particular setting. You might ask your students to use their senses to brainstorm the sounds, scents, images and so on that they associate with a particular place. You could also use poetry as part of the response after a trip to somewhere inspiring.

✓ *People*: Poetry offers an excellent form for describing a character in detail. Children and young people today live in a celebrity-obsessed world – ask them to write a poem about their favourite famous person. Alternatively, they might write a poem about someone they know well, perhaps their best friend, parent, or even (if you're feeling brave) their teacher.

✓ *Objects*: Just as an artist looks deeply at an object before and during the act of drawing it, so a poet can study something in detail with their words. When using an object for inspiration, start the lesson with a brainstorm of all the sensory words associated with it, as well as possible narratives connected to the object.

✓ *Other poets' work*: When approaching a particular topic in poetry, a good way into the work is to show your class samples of work by other poets on that subject, or of poets who write in a similar style to the one you'd like them to try.

The process of poetry

Writing poetry is as much about the process of writing as it is about the finished product. It can take longer to find inspiration for and to edit a poem effectively than it does to actually write the piece itself. It is tempting for students to write a poem straight off, and then declare it 'finished', without undergoing the processes that lead to a really powerful piece of work. However, if you can encourage your students to spend time working and reworking their poems, they will not only end up with a better finished product, but they will also be practising some of the most important writing skills.

Below are some suggestions about how you might prepare your children before they get down to the actual writing of a poem, and how you can encourage them to work and rework the piece once it is underway.

✓ *Brainstorming*: The brainstorm is tailor-made for the poetry writer, because it encourages us to pick out single striking images that may prove useful in the writing. For instance, a brainstorm on the word 'black cat' might bring out images to do with how the cat moves, looks and sounds. It might also inspire your students to think of other associations, such as witches, darkness and night.

✓ *Pick and mix*: After you've done a brainstorm with your students, write each word on a single card. Now shuffle the cards and hand out several to each group. Get the groups to arrange their cards in a 'word picture' (a poem!) and read it out to the class.

✓ *The senses*: Good poetry engages all the reader's senses. When you've found a topic for your students to work with, encourage them to think about how each of their senses might be involved. A good way to do this is to use a senses' worksheet. See the companion website for a downloadable version.

✓ *Sound*: As well as simply reading the words on the page (whether in the 'finished' poem or in the initial drafts), encourage your students to think about the sounds that their poetry is making and to read their work out loud. This might involve exploring alliterative effects within the piece, or it might be about onomatopoeic words and the impact that they have.

✓ *Cutting*: Often, the fewer words a poem has, the better and stronger the image it creates. When your students have 'finished' their piece, ask them to go back and see which words can be cut out. They might try cutting the total number of words in half, or simply removing any mundane or uninspiring vocabulary.

✓ *Structure*: When editing poetry, encourage your students to think about the way that the piece is structured, as well as the words it contains. This might involve dividing a poem up into verses, or laying it out in an interesting way on the page.

Motivating those who 'don't do poetry'

It is a pity that there are some students who just 'don't do' poetry, whether writing it or reading it. After all, 99.9 per cent of modern-day children love popular music, and what else is a song but poetry linked with music? I think this is the connection we are missing – a way of making poetry relevant to their everyday lives, rather than seeing it as something 'literary' and rather middle class.

Here are some thoughts about how you can motivate and engage those who believe that they have no interest in poems.

✓ *Appealing themes*: When working with poorly motivated students, find a theme or topic that is going to appeal. For instance, I once taught a class of GCSE students who were poorly motivated when it came to poetry. There was a high percentage of boys in the class, and I was determined to find some way of engaging their interest. I used a variety of poems on the subject of football, such as 'The ballad of Hillsborough' by Simon Rae, which caught their attention and proved to be motivating for them.

✓ *Well-known poems*: Students also engage with poems that they know well, or that they associate with a different medium, such as film. For instance, the poem 'Stop all the clocks', by W. H. Auden, appeared in the film *Four Weddings and a Funeral*. When I've used this piece to inspire my students in the past, they are delighted to find that they already know it from the film.

✓ *Appealing forms*: There is a great deal of what we would traditionally call poetry in modern-day musical forms, particularly in rap and hip-hop. These musical styles rely on the spoken word, with a strong rhythmic feel, and you can use this connection within the classroom as a motivator. Ask your students to bring in samples of their favourite tunes (although keep an eye out for inappropriate language). I have used the idea of rapping very effectively in the classroom when teaching iambic pentameter. By getting the class to 'rap' out the underlying beat on their desks, they gain a much better understanding of what this term is all about.

✓ *Songs as poetry*: Type out the lyrics of some popular songs and present them as 'poetry'. I once used this idea for a language-analysis lesson, in which I began by analysing the 'poems' (lyrics) with the class, and then showed them that these poems were in fact songs. We explored the tone of the poems as written pieces, and then looked at the way in which the music fitted (or didn't fit) the tone we had identified. This work could be followed up by asking your students to bring in songs of their own choice for inspiration and analysis.

✓ *Something shocking*: I will leave it up to you how far you are willing to go in employing 'shock tactics' (it depends a great deal on your school and the particular age of children that you teach). However, suffice to say that there are plenty of 'shocking' poems out there (in terms of both subject and language) that might well motivate students who are bored by conventional poetry.

✓ *Pure analysis*: Sometimes, the least-well-motivated students are engaged by the feeling that they are learning something highly technical and analytical. If this is the case with your class, introduce them to the delights of extended metaphors, pathetic fallacy, assonance, alliteration, and so on. You may well find that they surprise you in their level of interest.

And finally, get your students used to seeing poetry all over the place – encourage your school to see poetry as something that deserves a place on the corridor walls, in the toilets, in the hall, in the playground. Like the well loved idea of 'Poems on the Underground', find a place for poetry all around your school.

8

Non-fiction Writing

What is written without effort is in general read without pleasure.

Samuel Johnson

Non-fiction writing is a hard-won craft, as tough to do well as writing quality fiction or poetry. This chapter introduces you to a range of strategies and ideas for helping your students develop their non-fiction writing techniques, and write more effectively. I also look here at the key aspects of different types of non-fiction writing, such as writing to persuade or to instruct. I use the term 'non-fiction' to refer to the form or type of writing (instruction booklets, newspapers, writing to complain, and so on) as opposed to the content of or inspiration for the writing.

In many of the examples in this chapter, there is a creative basis for the content, but the students are asked to write as though this imaginary content is factual. Of course, non-fiction writing crops up in practically every area of the curriculum. I hope that teachers from all subject backgrounds will find some new ideas in this chapter to try out with their students.

Note-taking and annotation

For much non-fiction writing, students need to do research and take notes before they start to write, or analyse and annotate a text in preparation for writing about it. To do this well, they must understand how to identify the most important or relevant pieces of information, and how to note or highlight these so that they are easy to access at a later stage. Learning to pick out key points and take notes when the teacher is giving information orally is also a vital skill to learn.

To develop these key skills with your students:

✓ *Practise scanning texts*: Teach your students how to skim or speed read texts. Give a piece of text, and set a short amount of time to look through it. During this time (two or three minutes) students must pick out only the most important words. This forces them to utilize their visual reading ability, rather than spending time sounding out each word. They may be surprised at how straightforward this is to do.

✓ *Practise annotating texts*: There are lots of skills at work in this process – identifying important words or phrases, underlining or highlighting them, and showing why they are important. Model examples for and with your class.

✓ *Annotate step by step*: Take your students step by step through a piece of text. Give them a set of highlighters or coloured pens, then make notes on specific features of the text, one at a time. Show them how to write notes in the margin, how to use arrows, circling, underlining, and so on.

✓ *Work with listening as well as reading*: As well as taking notes from written texts, train your students to take notes from oral sources (you, or recordings of others). Model the process for them – read out a story or a piece of text, and pause so they can note down key words as you go along.

✓ *Use a concise and relevant layout*: Teach your students how to write notes so that they are easy to access in the future. Help them learn how to use brainstorms, mind-maps, etc.

✓ *Use colours*: Use colour to differentiate ideas that relate to different parts of a topic. Encourage your students to find their own creative, visual approaches to taking notes.

Texts for analysis

When analysing texts, include pieces that are topical or fun as well as more serious writing. Choose writing that will appeal to your students: a feature or article in a comic or magazine format, extracts from a book by Stephen King. Use your own writing as well – this is often the best way to show students a particular feature of writing, or a specific technique in use.

Right from the earliest moments, encourage your students to see texts as something to be picked apart, scribbled on, played around with. For instance, asking young students to underline the same words within a text, to explore the effect of repetition. Make 'working with texts' an active process, one that helps your students develop their own writing. Demystify the world of books and writing, and pull down some of the barriers that stand between the reluctant writer and the text.

Building your writing

Many students view writing in the same way that they experience reading: they should start to write at the beginning of a text and keep moving forwards until they get to the end. But there is of course a huge difference between reading a finished piece of text and creating your own writing. The writer of the text being read will have spent substantial amounts of time constructing it; this is what you should encourage your students to do as well.

As an author, a large part of the process of writing my books actually involves 'building' them. I start with an outline of what the book might include, and gradually fill in this outline and develop the book, moving chunks, cutting excess, tweaking here and there. Computers make this constructing and editing process much simpler, both for me, and for your students.

To give a metaphorical example, building your writing is much the same as building a house. You start with the 'big picture', the overall design of the piece, and then gradually construct the frame and begin to add the walls. It is only when the building is complete that the 'finishing touches' can be added. Your students should 'build' their writing using the processes described in this chapter and in Chapter 3. Share this metaphor with your students, to help them understand exactly what is involved. Find a detailed description of the processes to download and share with your class at the companion website.

Frames and structures

Some students find it simple to work out the appropriate structure for their writing; others really struggle, and need the teacher to model and scaffold the writing with and for them. You can find more on frames and frameworks in Chapter 3 (p. 45). When using writing frames, encourage your students to identify the relevant features for themselves, rather than always providing them with a ready-made framework. This creates ownership of the ideas, and helps them develop their analytical skills.

For instance, you might look at a series of letters together, identifying the aspects and features that appear in each one, and applying these to their own work. Similarly, you might read a number of recipes with your class and explore the way they are structured, and the elements that must be included. These details could be brainstormed in groups, then annotated on the board for the whole class to use. Again, it's about learning to break writing down, in order to see the techniques and strategies that the writer uses.

Non-fiction forms

When writing factual pieces, for instance in history, geography or science, be inventive with the forms you use, especially if your students need motivating. For instance, use the newspaper form to write about a historical event, or the recipe form to write out a chemistry experiment. These forms have the potential to be used in non-fiction writing across the curriculum:

✓ summaries
✓ newspaper stories
✓ reviews
✓ reports
✓ detailed analysis
✓ essays
✓ brochures and pamphlets
✓ programmes
✓ manuals
✓ instruction booklets
✓ recipes
✓ shopping lists
✓ letters
✓ emails
✓ web pages
✓ diaries
✓ news reports
✓ police reports
✓ witness statements
✓ TV programmes
✓ magazines, including:
   – articles
   – problem pages
   – letters pages
   – advertisements.

Technique and non-fiction writing

In non-fiction writing the word 'technique' applies to the accuracy of the spelling, punctuation and grammar, but it also applies to the technique of structuring the writing, or of drafting and editing it. Two of the key techniques you want your students to develop in their non-fiction writing are rhythm and tone. These make the difference between an average piece of non-fiction writing, and one that is good or outstanding.

Rhythm in non-fiction writing

Although we might traditionally associate rhythm with poetry, all good writing has an internal rhythm of its own. It's like listening to a charismatic and engaging speaker – you are engaged as much by how they sound as by what they are saying. When rhythm is used effectively, the writing flows naturally, and sounds right to the reader. Where rhythm is not well used, the writing sounds clunky or forced, and it is hard for the reader to relax into the writing.

The rhythm of writing is made up of a range of components: the sound and length of the words used; the way that the sentences and paragraphs are structured; the type of connecting words that are used, and so on. Learning to 'hear' how your own writing sounds (preferably as you write it) is a technique that develops with time and practice.

Help your students develop their use of rhythm by:

✓ *'Hearing' their writing*: Ask students to read work out loud, to the class or to a partner, or to record it. Encourage them to develop that silent internal voice as well, the one that speaks to us as we write – when writing in exams, your students cannot hear their writing read out loud.

✓ *Developing grammatical structures*: Where writers have a limited vocabulary and understanding of technique, the rhythm is stilted: the basic single clause structure of subject – verb – object. 'The girl – threw – the ball.' As your students develop an understanding of more complex grammatical structures, their writing can start to flow. Experiment with different effects:

   – Insert a short phrase into the middle of an existing sentence: 'The girl, / who was really good at sport, / threw the ball.'
   – Brainstorm a variety of verbs: 'The girl chucked / lobbed / flung / heaved the ball.'
   – Develop descriptive techniques: 'The girl threw the old, threadbare ball.'
   – Use imagery, for instance personification: 'The girl threw the ball, and it flew triumphantly into the net.'

✓ *Using punctuation*: The way that a writer punctuates her work has a strong impact on its rhythm. For instance, if a long sentence is broken up with lots of commas, this slows the reader down, forcing him to take breaths, as the sentence you have just read demonstrates. Similarly, the use of questions and exclamation marks also affects the rhythm of a piece of writing, because it creates pauses and emphasis.

✓ *Playing with vocabulary*: Some words create a strong emphasis within a sentence, causing the reader to pause. These can be long words, with several syllables, which simply take longer to read. Alternatively they can be emotive ones – words that conjure up strong images: 'horrific', 'extraordinary' or 'terrifying'.

✓ *Using presentational devices*: Italics and bold have an impact on the rhythm and stresses within a piece of writing. If the reader sees the word *horrific*, he stresses it even more strongly because it appears in italics.

✓ *Mixing sentence lengths*: A piece of writing with a good rhythm generally has mixed sentence lengths. Short sentences can be used to develop tension or pace, or to give the piece a feeling of simplicity and clarity. Student writers often use a long sentence when a couple of shorter ones would in fact work better. Experiment with breaking down longer sentences into shorter, pithier ones. What is the effect on the rhythm of the piece?

✓ *'Notating' the writing*: To analyse the rhythm or metre of poetry, we break down each line into syllables and stresses. You can do this with narrative and non-fiction writing, for instance counting the number of words and syllables in each sentence, to identify the rhythm being used. Experiment with notating writing as though it were a musical score, to explore the overall pattern of the words. How many 'beats' (syllables) are there in each word or phrase? Which words create a heavy 'beat' (emphasis)? Is the writing 'staccato' (choppy) or 'legato' (flowing)?

Tone in non-fiction writing

The appropriate tone for non-fiction writing depends on the reason behind the writing, and on the audience being addressed. Being able to write with an effective tone is closely connected to finding a voice in your writing. For instance, when writing to complain about something, the writer might want to sound indignant or shocked. When writing to instruct, the writer would probably use a calm, unemotional, direct tone of voice. There are various ways in which your students can add tone to their writing. Many of the factors that influence rhythm will also have an effect on tone.

Encourage your students to experiment with:

✓ *A variety of words*: A great deal of tone can be created just by using the right vocabulary. Find a bank of words to use for different types of writing. For instance, when writing to complain, they might be 'concerned', 'horrified', or 'astounded'.

✓ *The use of questions*: A question, especially within non-fiction writing, creates a very particular tone. The question might be rhetorical, or it could be a direct question to the reader/audience. It might be asked with a horrified tone, or as a simple query. Using questions tends to slow down or pause the reader, as he considers what his answer would be. Using questions also creates a connection between writer and reader – the writer is directly addressing his audience.

✓ *Limited use of exclamation marks*: Exclamation marks are useful for indicating a shocking fact or belief, when used in limited numbers. However, one of the hallmarks of the inexperienced writer is feeling the need to use punctuation marks to put across tone. The use of exclamation marks is usefully described as being 'like laughing at your own jokes'. More than one in any single piece of non-fiction writing is probably too many.

✓ *The use of statements*: Making statements should be done with care in non-fiction writing, especially if the subject being discussed is controversial, or is not generally considered as 'fact'. The overuse of statements creates rather a pompous tone, as though the writer believes that what she says is always right. Encourage your students to experiment with using interpretations rather than statements. This will help them create different tones within their writing. It is also useful for those awkward examination moments when they are unsure if that 'fact' they vaguely remember is 100 per cent correct or not. Phrases for suggesting, rather than stating, include:
  – It could be argued that ...
  – Some people believe ...
  – One interpretation of this is ...
  – Several commentators have observed that ...

✓ *The use of italic/bold*: Putting a word or phrase in italics or bold has an impact on rhythm, and creates a strong and emphatic tone. These presentational devices should be used sparingly, rather than being scattered throughout the writing. In fact, a writer with a powerful enough sense of voice can give emphasis mainly through vocabulary and structure.

Types of non-fiction writing

It is vital to understand the reason for any piece of non-fiction writing, because this helps us work out the appropriate form, tone, structure, presentation, grammatical features and vocabulary to use for this particular audience. The question 'What am I trying to achieve with this piece of writing?' is fundamental to making writing effective.

But there is a double layer of purpose within the writing tasks you set. While your purpose is to teach your students the correct form, tone, structure and so on to use, you also need to give *them* a purpose for learning about these things. If they're going to feel motivated, they need a reason to write that piece of non-fiction, preferably one beyond 'you've got to learn how to write a letter of complaint because it's in the curriculum'.

This is where an imaginative context for non-fiction writing comes into play. For instance, you present the class with a letter of complaint from the people who live in the house next to the school. They are complaining bitterly about the levels of noise in the playground at playtimes. The students must write a letter of response, to persuade the neighbours about why playtime is so important.

For each piece of non-fiction writing, you and your students need to consider:

- What do I want to communicate?
- What's the reason behind writing this?
- What form is it most appropriate for me to use?
- Who or what is the audience for this piece?
- What will this audience expect from my writing?
- How formal does my style of writing need to be?
- What response am I hoping to receive?

Let's look now at the six main types of non-fiction writing. For each type of writing, you'll find information on:

- the purpose of this type of writing
- the forms in which this writing is usually found
- the kind of structure that is typically used for this writing
- the key features found within this writing
- some useful language tips and commonly found words and phrases
- ideas for teaching this type of writing
- an example of an activity that you could try with your students.

Recount (account)

Purpose: Recounts and accounts are used to write about events that have happened. Most stories use this type of writing. The main purpose is typically to inform and entertain the reader, but this can vary according to the genre involved.

Forms: Write-up of a trip, activity or visit, story, diary entry, journal, newspaper report, letter.

Structure

–   A paragraph of orientation – which sets the scene and lets the reader know where they are.
–   An account of the events that happened, typically in chronological order.
–   A 'reorientation', referring back to the original setting ('It was a wonderful trip and I hope to go back there again very soon').
–   Or a summary of the events, or some kind of concluding paragraph.

Key features

–   A recount is usually written in the past tense, because it describes something that has already happened.
–   However, the present tense can be used for more informal recounts and for effect: 'So, I'm waiting for the bus when suddenly my friend drives past.'
–   Although it's usually written in chronological order, the writer might use flashbacks to play around with the sequence of events.
–   There's often a personal element to the recount, which may take the form of an anecdote.
–   Typically, a single person or group of people are the subject of the piece.
–   The writer typically uses 'I' or 'we' to describe what happened.

Useful language tips

✓ Recounts often use time connectives – first, then, next, immediately after – to show the sequence of events.
✓ Recounts should be factual and subjective, so avoid the use of adjectives and adverbs in non-fiction recounts.

Ideas for teaching

✓ Get your students to use a timeline, to help them work out the best way to order their recount of events.

✓ Alternatively, use a flowchart to help them plan the sequence of events.

✓ Encourage them to experiment with using flashbacks, to add interest to their pieces. When describing a trip, what would the effect be if they moved one of the middle paragraphs to the beginning?

✓ Get your students to add in plenty of details, by encouraging them to ask questions about who, what, where, when and why.

Example

A diary entry about 'The last day on Earth'. Give your students a sentence with which to start their recount: 'As I sit here waiting for the asteroid to hit, I take a moment to think about what I did during *the last day on Earth*.' For added inspiration you might like to read them the story *The Last Night of the World* by Ray Bradbury.

Report (non-chronological)

Purpose: A report gives factual details on a subject or topic, or describes what things are or were like.

Form: Guidebook, encyclopaedia entry, catalogue, leaflet, article, non-fiction book, letter.

Structure

– A report will typically open with a statement which describes the subject of the report.

– The length of a report will depend on the audience and on the form of writing.

– A report may well include a summary of the main features of the subject, perhaps as a list of bullet points or in a diagram.

Key features

– A report is written in the present tense, although it can include references to or be about the past, in which case it would use the past tense.

- It is written in the third person, and using mainly a formal and impersonal style.
- Reports are not written in chronological order.
- They may include illustrations and diagrams.
- A report gives details about the qualities of its subject, such as its parts, functions, habits and behaviours.
- The subject of a report will typically be generic – frogs, the Romans, Paris – rather than specific.
- If appropriate, the writer can use tables, diagrams and images to illustrate the subject further or more fully.
- The title of the report is typically related to the subject, e.g. 'Roman coins'.

Useful language tips

✓ A report uses precise and descriptive language.
✓ It should be easy to read and understand, and suited to the type and age of audience who will be reading it.
✓ Where there is more complicated language, this is technical language relating to the subject itself.

Ideas for teaching

✓ Encourage your students to use questions to engage the reader's interest. These might be in the title, or in the body of the text: 'Have you ever wondered how Roman coins were made?'
✓ Experiment with writing the same report, for different audiences. For instance, an encyclopaedia entry for a children's version, and the same entry for a GCSE exam.

Example
The students are asked to imagine that they work for a famous footballer. The footballer is going to join a new club overseas, and wants them to write a report about the new city he will live in. The report should be tailored to this specific audience – include information about the local press, nightlife, shopping, and some useful phrases in the new language.

Explanation

Purpose: An explanation will answer a question, explain how things are, how something works or why something happens.

Forms: Manual, textbook, question and answer writing, leaflets, encyclopaedia.

Structure

- An explanation starts with a general statement about what the writer is going to explain, introducing the topic to the reader.
- This is followed by each of a series of logical steps to be taken, or to explain how something works or why it happens.
- A summary is used to conclude the explanation.

Key features

- An explanation typically uses the simple present tense.
- The title links to what is being explained – 'The life cycle of the frog'.
- An explanation may include some images or diagrams, which are labelled to show how they work.
- It should include interesting details and facts about the subject.

Useful language tips

✓ An explanation might use both temporal connectives – first, then, after that – and causal connectives – because, so, therefore.
✓ The writer could speak directly to the reader – 'You might be surprised to discover that …'

Ideas for teaching

✓ Use a writing frame to help younger or less-able students write an explanation. The frame you use will be specific to the subject or the topic of the piece.
✓ For instance, an explanation of the life cycle of the frog might be framed by temporal connectives: 'In early spring …', 'later on in spring …'

Example
The Year 7 students are asked to write a Q&A style leaflet for the children in year 6 in local schools. The leaflet should provide an explanation of what secondary school is like, what they need to bring with them, and include some commonly asked questions (FAQs).

Instructions (procedure)

Purpose: Instructions, or sets of procedures, are designed to show people how to do or make something, via a step-by-step guide.

Forms: Posters, notices, signs, technical 'step by step' manuals, DIY book, instructions, recipes, experiments, sewing patterns, rules for a game.

Structure
- First, the goal of the instructions is defined, perhaps as a title – 'Instructions to make a ...'
- Next comes a list of what is needed (equipment, etc.) in the order it will be used.
- This is followed by a sequence of steps, again in the order that they should be done.
- The final sentences will wrap up the set of procedures: 'Let your cake cool. Now eat and enjoy!'

Key features
- Instructions will often be written as a set of bullet points or a numbered list.
- The title links to what the text is about – 'How to construct your bookshelves'.
- Instructions often use lots of diagrams to clarify meaning. These are sometimes used instead of text – 'see the diagram on page 5'.
- The sentences will usually be short.
- There might be an appeal to the reader: 'Everyone loves this game.'

Useful language tips

✓ Instructions use clear and simple language; the writer will often try to make them sound easy to follow ('only four simple steps'). Typically, they are anything but easy to follow in reality!

✓ The writer will only use adverbs or adjectives if needed for clarity ('the blue wire').

✓ Instructions typically use imperative verbs, which insist that the reader does something – 'cut the wire', 'open the packet'.

✓ There may also be negative commands, to keep the reader on track – 'Do not join points A and B together yet'.

✓ Instructions will often include time connectives – 'First', 'then', 'now'.

Ideas for teaching

✓ Get your students to experiment with formal and informal language in their instructions. What are the different effects, for instance, if we place, pop or even shove a cake in the oven?

> **Example**
> Get your students to write instructions to do something simple (e.g. tie up their shoes) but without actually doing that thing. Swap instructions with a partner; they have to follow them. Did it work?

Persuasive writing

Purpose: To encourage the reader (or viewer) to do or believe something – this may be by covert as well as by overt methods. Writing to complain is a form of persuasive writing, where the writer tries to persuade the reader that a problem has occurred.

Forms: Advert, letter applying for a job, political leaflet, pamphlet from a pressure group, letter of complaint, poster, book blurb, catalogue, travel brochure.

Structure

– An opening statement is given to sum up the writer's position.
– The writer presents the general details of his viewpoint or standpoint and then develops these.
– A closing statement is given which reinforces the position.

Note: adverts may dispense with this structure, and many of the key features below, using images rather than text to convey meaning and to persuade.

Key features

- Only one side of the argument is presented – material is selected to support that particular view.
- The simple present tense is used.
- There's often a combination of media – for instance photos alongside the text of an advert.
- Depending on the form, topic and audience, the writer may need to appear reasonable and unbiased, rather than emotive.
- In other situations, the writer can use heavily emotive language – 'The whole world is threatened by the potentially devastating impact of climate change ...'
- Typically, persuasive writing uses positive, rather than negative, language.
- The writer addresses the reader directly – 'This new computer is just what you've been waiting for!'
- Persuasive writing appeals to the reader's judgement and discernment, to try to get her onside – 'As a discerning customer, we feel sure you will love ...'
- Facts, figures and research may be used to convince the reader that this viewpoint is correct: 'At least eight out of ten dogs love Chum Chum biscuits'.

Useful language tips

- ✓ Logical connectives are often included to back up the writer's point – 'this proves that', 'so it's clear that', 'so you'll agree with me that'.
- ✓ Alliteration is popular in advertising, to make slogans memorable, and to make the language trip off the tongue.
- ✓ The writer may ask rhetorical questions of her reader, to draw her in and make her feel that she is being appealed to personally.
- ✓ Persuasive words include: obviously, clearly, I strongly believe that, do you really think, do you want to be part of, I was shocked to find.
- ✓ In advertising campaigns, a slogan will often be created as a memorable 'hook' for the audience.

Ideas for teaching

- ✓ It works well to get your students to argue a position that is the polar opposite to what they actually believe. For instance, on a topic such as animal experimentation, they must argue for the scientists' position, if they believe the opposite.

✓ Come up with some 'hot topics' of your own, by creating fictions where something at school is going to change. See below for one suggestion.

> **Example**
> The teacher writes a persuasive letter to the head, saying why playtime should be cut by 50 per cent to improve behaviour in the school. She shows this to the class and pretends that she is deadly serious about it – she is sure that she will convince the head. The students have to write their own letters to try and persuade the head teacher otherwise.

Discussion

Purpose: To show the reader both sides of an argument, with accompanying evidence, and possibly also to conclude which is correct.

Forms: Debates, essays, leaflets, non-fiction books.

Structure

- An introduction which gives a statement about the issue being discussed.
- A paragraph (or several paragraphs) outlining one side of the the argument, and giving supporting reasons, evidence, and/or examples.
- A paragraph (or several paragraphs) outlining the other side of argument, again with supporting reasons, evidence and/or examples.
- A summary, which might include a conclusion about which side is right, and give supporting evidence as to why the writer believes this.

Key features

- Discursive texts use the simple present tense.
- They tend to be about generalized groups – 'some people', 'most scientists'.
- Generic statements are followed by specific examples. At a higher level, the ideas are developed as in the four step essay-writing technique described in Chapter 6 (p. 105).

– Generally speaking, the writer is unemotional about the subject, and writes in an impersonal way.

Useful language tips

✓ The language indicates that the writer is taking an unbiased viewpoint, and presenting both sides of the argument – 'Some people believe that ...', 'on the other hand ...'

✓ The writer might also be asked to 'compare and contrast', in other words to find common features, and also those aspects that differ widely.

Ideas for teaching

✓ Chapter 6 gives an in-depth exploration of the techniques involved in writing discursive texts.

✓ When giving both sides of an argument or situation, it's useful to get your students to do a table. They can use this to compare the opposing viewpoints and to help them find examples for each side.

Example

Set the class a topic to debate, for instance: 'University tuition should be free for everyone.' Now ask the students to split into two groups, depending on whether they are for or against the statement. The groups should work together to discuss and brainstorm ideas for their side, to give in a debate. Give each group a stack of postcards – they write down their ideas, one per postcard. Now there's a twist. The groups swap over the set of postcards. A debate is held, in which the students must argue the opposing team's viewpoint.

The importance of being an expert

The 'role of the expert' is a drama technique that can be used to great effect when working on non-fiction writing. By creating the fiction that your students are a group of experts on a particular subject, and giving them the power that goes along with this role, you will find amazing levels of motivation are achieved. The students love being taken 'out of' the school setting and put into a fictional scenario in which they have power and influence.

When using the role of experts for non-fiction writing, I have found that one of the best approaches is to use a group project. This allows each member of the group to utilize their own particular abilities and talents, and also to learn from the people that they are working with. I have used this type of 'experts project' very successfully when working with targeted, lower-ability groups, as well as with more-able students. You can find some advice below about how to use the 'role of the expert' in your own classroom.

Running a group project

Before setting up and running a group project like this, there are various technical and organizational issues that you should address. The points below are gathered from my experience of actually using these projects within my classroom.

✓ *Group numbers*: The best number for a group project is about four students. Much more than this, and the groups find it hard to work together and to stay organized. Less than this, and you miss out on the different areas of skill that each student brings to the work.

✓ *Group mixes*: Group projects offer us an excellent opportunity for mixed ability work. The more able should help out their less-able counterparts; the quieter students should keep the over-confident 'leaders' in check.

✓ *Choice of groups*: Students tend to work best if they choose their own groups, working with people that they like. However, this can lead to wasted time spent on social chatter. If you allow your students to choose the make-up of their groups, ensure that the less popular or quieter ones are not left out. Consider using random groupings if you've got a tricky class.

✓ *Timescale*: It is important to set a timescale before beginning this type of work. Otherwise, the project tends to expand to fit the amount of time you are willing to give it. Set a realistic timescale and give your class targets for each lesson's work to help keep them on track.

✓ *Setting the focus*: To keep the class on task, write out a worksheet with a series of activities you want them to complete. The group can then divide these activities up so that each person has a specific task on which to focus.

✓ *Keeping the focus*: It often happens that the students lose their focus, spending excessive amounts of time on an area of the project that they particularly enjoy. To avoid this problem, ask your students to agree specific activities that they will complete during each lesson, and also to set themselves homework tasks.

✓ *Audience*: For most of the projects suggested below, there is a specific audience for the work. Make the audience as real as possible, for instance selling the magazine (see below) to other students within the school. This will motivate your students to produce their best work.

✓ *Presentation*: Do try to give your students the opportunity to present at least some of their work on the computer. This helps them produce a 'finished product' of which they can be proud.

Ideas for group projects

Below are some suggestions for 'role of the expert' projects across the curriculum. These ideas could be adapted to use with students across the primary and secondary age range.

✓ *The personnel managers' dilemma*: The students work as personnel managers, and they have to decide how to save money for their company. This might be achieved by sacking some staff, or in another, more lateral way (it's up to them how they do it). The groups are given a list of staff, with details about their work backgrounds, experience, qualifications, home life and so on. They must consult together to choose what to do, writing a report on their findings, and presenting their ideas to the class. I have used this project in English lessons, but it could also prove useful for business studies, maths or citizenship work.

✓ *The pop group*: The students work in a group, playing the role of the manager of a pop group. They must work on all the different tasks for their group: from writing song lyrics to making a CD cover, from designing posters for a tour to writing a fanzine for the band.

✓ *The magazine*: For many students, much of their day-to-day reading will be of magazines – on football, music, fashion, computer games. When setting a group project to make a magazine you can choose from a huge range of different subject areas, depending on the area of the curriculum.

Writing about language

Analysing and writing about the way that other writers use language helps our students to develop a greater understanding of their own work. The analysis of both simple and complex texts can teach us a great deal, and this study can begin at an early age. For instance, with young children we might explore how the instructions for a children's board game are written, whilst with older students we might look at the ways in which advertisers appeal to their market. This analysis of language use can take place across the curriculum: for instance getting your students to study the way a scientific report is written before writing one of their own.

There are various things to consider when studying and writing about language. Here are some questions that you might find useful:

- What type of audience is this piece of writing aimed at?
- What age are the audience?
- What type of people are the audience?
- How does the intended audience affect the way that the piece is written?
- What form is the writing in?
- Why has this particular form been used?
- What viewpoint is being used (i.e. first or third person)?
- What sort of vocabulary is used?
- How simple or complicated is the vocabulary and sentence structure?
- How long is each word or sentence?
- Is the writing difficult or easy to understand?
- How formal or informal is the writing?
- How is the piece structured – what is in each paragraph and why?
- How does the writing start and finish?
- What point or points is the writer trying to make?
- Is the writer trying to convince us of a particular point of view? Do they succeed?
- What tone does the writer use?
- Is the writer feeling a certain emotion or mood?
- Does the writer use any linguistic devices within the piece?
- How is the piece of writing laid out on the page?
- Are there any special presentational devices used, such as different fonts or text sizes?
- Do you find this piece of writing interesting or engaging? Why? Why not?
- What techniques does the writer use that you might be able to transfer into your own writing?

Writing about literature

In the same way that studying and writing about language use can help us develop our own writing, so looking at literature in detail can be very beneficial for our creative work. The closeness of the connection between the acts of reading and writing means that even the youngest students can make a simple analysis of the way that books work. By studying the way that authors write, we can help both the youngest and the oldest students to develop their own writing.

Encourage your students to 'read as a writer and write as a reader'. Look for extracts from literature that will inspire and engage them; comedy, horror, science fiction, as well as the set texts that you are required to study.

Checklist for analysing literature

– Imagery and language devices: simile, metaphor, personification, repetition, pathetic fallacy.
– Vocabulary choice: length of words, type of words, emotive, descriptive, subjective.
– Sentence structure and patterns.
– The rhythm of the language.
– Viewpoint – where the writer stands in relation to the reader, unreliable narrators.
– Paragraphing and layout.
– Characterization.
– How setting and atmosphere are created.
– Plot devices: back story, flashbacks, slow motion, close observation.
– Tension – conflict, dramatic irony.

9

Writing in the Digital Age

Computers have lots of memory but no imagination.

Author unknown

This chapter looks at the subject of writing in the digital age, exploring ways in which ICT can be used to motivate your students and help them develop their writing. I also deal with the advantages and disadvantages of using computers as a teaching tool, and examine how you might use resources such as the internet and email. When using ICT in the classroom, bear in mind that your students may well know as much or more about computers than you do. The digital age has happened suddenly. The current generation of children and young people grew up with the technology, whereas some teachers might not have had access to the most basic computers during their own schooling. Utilize the knowledge that your students have, and if there are experts on different aspects of ICT in your classroom, get them to help teach you and the rest of your class.

To some people, writing on a computer seems like 'cheating': they feel that computers make the writer lazy, that they do all the work, checking spelling and grammar and offering an electronic thesaurus. Whilst computers should never replace the need for students to learn and practise longhand writing, we must embrace the advantages that using ICT can bring. At the same time we must bear in mind its potential disadvantages, and learn to mitigate these for our students. The ever-increasing use of technology means that writing becomes more important, not less. The internet allows people from all over the world to publish their ideas and their writing in a public forum for anyone to access. As teachers and writers, we should celebrate this fact.

ICT and writing

As a teacher you need to make choices about how and when writing on computers is going to happen in your classroom. You'll also need to think about how processes such as research, brainstorming and planning might fit into the digital format. There are various different approaches you can use. Each one has its own value as a learning tool. Utilize the one that you feel will work best for that particular bit of the lesson or topic.

Depending on the access you have to computers, you might have a full set of laptops in your own classroom, you could be taking a whole class into a room where there are plenty of computers, or you could be setting them off in a small groups to work on a limited range of machines.

Your students could:

✓ brainstorm, plan and map out their ideas first on paper, then type up the finished piece on a computer
✓ work together with the teacher to gather ideas straight onto an interactive whiteboard (both the teacher and the students can write the ideas up), then use this initial planning stage to inform longhand writing
✓ type up a piece of finished written work on the computer, to learn more about presentational techniques, for instance creating a leaflet
✓ write a piece from start to finish on a computer or laptop, for instance creating a PowerPoint presentation to teach something to the rest of the class
✓ work backwards – read sample texts onscreen, and then use these to inform a piece of longhand writing
✓ use ICT for researching facts, information or ideas, to make notes or write a piece of text longhand
✓ communicate with other students via the written word
✓ celebrate their written work by publishing it online.

Advantages

The secret of effective ICT use in the classroom is to consider the advantages that it brings, and to maximize these for our students. It is tempting to see ICT as simply a tool for students to present their writing to you and the class. However, their use goes way beyond simply producing 'pretty' pieces of text.

✓ *A building tool*: Word-processing and other presentational software offers the writer a wonderful degree of flexibility. You can build a basic outline of a piece first, then fill in the gaps bit by bit, elaborating on each idea in turn. This initial outline acts as a useful plan, indicating the order in which the ideas will come, where the paragraph or page breaks should be, and so on.

✓ *An editing tool*: ICT allows us to edit our work with remarkable ease. We can cut out whole sections, move a paragraph from the beginning to the end of a piece of writing, change single words, alter sentence structure, and so on, all without taking much effort or time. Before the computer, such changes would have meant hours of work in rewriting by hand.

✓ *A presentational device*: Giving your students the opportunity to produce a finished and beautifully presented piece of writing is highly motivating for them. Good presentation is also very pleasing for teachers and parents, and is useful when you want to display your students' writing. Presenting work on the computer is not just about printing out beautifully word-processed written assignments, it can also encompass the use of programs such as PowerPoint, which allow children to create a 'live' presentation of their writing.

✓ *Presenting worksheets*: Computers also offer an excellent way for teachers to present worksheets for the class. Time spent on creating engaging and exciting worksheets can be very useful in motivating your students. Because copying and editing are so easy, we can make minor changes to differentiate these worksheets. A worksheet stored on the computer can also be easily accessed, updated and printed out. You can also find literally thousands of worksheets online, to download, adapt and use.

✓ *Help for those with special education needs (SEN)*: For those students who have special needs, using a computer to write is an excellent way of building confidence. For instance, a student who finds spelling incredibly difficult can have his worries eased by the use of a spellchecker.

✓ *Help with technical accuracy*: Computers allow us to write with a high degree of technical accuracy. Although computers should not replace the need for learning proper technique, spelling and grammar checkers provide a useful tool for identifying areas of difficulty.

✓ *Help for those with poor handwriting*: Writing on a computer is also helpful for those who find neat or legible handwriting a challenge. Again, although the teacher clearly needs to work with these students on developing and improving their handwriting, using a computer allows them to produce and present a piece of 'finished' work.

✓ *A wealth of data*: The internet offers your students a wealth of source material to inspire and inform their writing. It has opened up written material to the masses and allowed writers around the world to communicate with each other.

✓ *A tool for celebrating and communicating*: ICT offers you a brilliant way to share ideas with the wider community, and to celebrate the writing that your own students have done.

Disadvantages

Just as we should learn to maximize the advantages of computers for written tasks, so we also need to be aware of the disadvantages. By being conscious of these, we can take steps to avoid any pitfalls.

✗ *The potential for distraction*: When writing on a computer, it is easy to get distracted from the task in hand. Even with filtering software, there are so many different internet sites, and it is so easy to click from one link to another, that a substantial amount of time can go by without anything concrete being achieved. Similarly, many students will spend a lot of time playing with different fonts and text colours, rather than concentrating on the content of their writing. Although this might be one of your learning objectives for a presentation task, it can take up a disproportionate amount of time.

✗ *The potential for laziness*: Although spelling and grammar checkers are very useful, there is the potential for students to use them mindlessly, without considering why and where they are making mistakes.

✗ *An easy sense of achievement*: When working on a computer, there is often the sense that you have achieved something, simply because the work looks good. Teachers, as well as students, need to be aware that content is what really matters, no matter how beautifully presented the piece of work might be.

✗ *The potential for plagiarism*: Electronic encyclopaedias, and of course the internet, make it annoyingly easy for students to 'cheat' in their writing. Fortunately, this plagiarism is often easy to spot, because the student does not make any attempt to hide the original source. You can also use special software to detect plagiarism. See the companion website for details.

✗ *Computers never lie*: Technology seduces us into believing that everything we read onscreen is the truth. This applies particularly to the internet – it is easy to be convinced that websites are factual and accurate, whilst this may not be the case. Word-processing programs are often set up to default to American spelling and grammar, so this should be switched to the English version.

✗ *Sometimes we need to break the rules*: Sometimes writers break grammatical rules on purpose, to achieve a certain tone or effect in their writing. If your students rely totally on what a grammar check tells them, it narrows down the possibilities for 'breaking the rules' and consequently for achieving some more interesting effects in their writing.

✗ *Availability of resources*: Many teachers face a situation where there are just not enough computers or laptops available, or where access to the internet is slow or unreliable. These factors need to be taken into account when planning for writing using ICT.

✗ *Over-editing*: Although one of the wonderful aspects of using a computer is the ability to edit without hours of rewriting by hand, this aspect also has its downside, in that it is often too easy for our students to edit their work. They go on and on fiddling with the piece, long beyond the point at which improvements are being made. With every piece of writing, there must come a point at which it is 'finished'.

✗ *'Typing up'*: There is the temptation to use word-processing programs for typing up handwritten pieces of work, rather than as a tool for building pieces of writing.

✗ *The '10 per cent rule'*: The majority of us (me included) use only a fraction of the functions available in our software programs – one estimate is an amazing 10 per cent! There are many tools to which we remain completely oblivious, probably because many of us learn 'on the job' and are not specifically trained in ICT.

✗ *Safety issues*: When using the internet, there are inevitably lots of issues around students' safety. See the detailed section later on in this chapter.

Word processing

It's amazing to think that there are plenty of teachers (myself included) who can remember a time before personal computers and laptops were commonly available, either in the home or in schools and workplaces. These days, it's taken for granted that we can type a text onscreen, edit it, print it, send it to someone else.

When teaching writing, one of your key ICT tools will be the use of word-processing software. In this section you can find lots of tips about how to overcome the common issues and errors, and also how to use word processing more effectively for writing activities. If you'd like some 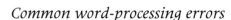 more advice about useful word-processing functions for your students to use, visit the companion website for a whole section on this topic.

Common word-processing errors

Because so much written work takes place using a word-processing program it's sensible to consider some of the more common errors that your students might make, and how these might be avoided. Although they are relatively simple ideas, the errors listed below are ones that I have seen from countless numbers of students over the years. Many of these errors are only highlighted when editing writing onscreen: it looks fine to start with, but once the student begins to move things around, all the mistakes become apparent. When you're using computers as a writing tool, spend time teaching your class how to use the functions correctly. Don't assume that they know how to do it correctly.

✘ *Space-bar fever*: The student with 'space-bar fever' fails to make any use of the left/right and centre alignment functions. They also completely ignore the tab button. Over the years I have watched many students with their thumb pressed hard down on the space bar in order to centre or right align their text. Explain to them how simple the computer makes it for us to layout our work.

✘ *Wrap around disease*: Similarly, I have often been presented with strange-looking pieces of writing, in which the student has used the return key at the end of a line, rather than allowing the text to wrap around automatically. This might not be apparent at first glance, but soon becomes a problem when the student edits the work and the new lines appear in the middle of the page.

✘ *New page*: In Microsoft Word, the shortcut for adding a new page is Ctrl+Return. Students often add a number of returns in order to move onto a new page – a mistake that only becomes obvious when they try to change the order of their writing.

✘ *Blank pages*: When checking through a student's work before it is sent to print, I have often come across a series of blank pages at the end of a document. My theory is that these appear because the student overuses the return key (see above). Do encourage your students to delete these blank pages before printing – otherwise you will find hundreds of clear white sheets spewing out of your printer.

✘ *What's in a name?* The name that they give their documents might seem trivial to your students, but there is little more frustrating than not being able to find that masterpiece of wordprocessing that they spent an hour on in the last lesson. Encourage your students to find sensible and informative names for their documents. The best document names give some indication of the content of the writing, and also perhaps a hint of the writer's name. This problem can be further overcome by getting your students to set up an individual folder on the computer in which to save their work. Alternatively, use a list of numbered texts (story001, story002) and keep a separate list of what each number represents.

Top tips for effective wordprocessing

I am fortunate in having worked with computers in an office long before I became a teacher. I was trained to word-process documents, and I also learned how to touch-type. In fact I would advise any teacher who has the time, opportunity or inclination to learn how to type properly. Being able to touch-type makes creating worksheets a far quicker task, and is also very useful when it comes to writing computerized reports. It also makes a nifty magic trick to show your classes – every student who has ever seen me type without looking at my fingers asks 'How on earth do you do that?'

Encourage your students to learn to touch-type as well – it will save them from years of two-fingered 'pecking' at the keyboard. Although in the initial stages it takes a while to learn, in the long run they will save vast amounts of time. There are loads of touch-typing programmes available online. A good starting point is the BBC's www.bbc.co.uk/schools/typing/.

Here are my three top tips to help you and your students use word processing more effectively:

✓ *Write first, format last*: It is incredibly tempting for students to spend vast quantities of time 'prettying up' their work as they write: changing fonts and text sizes, adding colours and shading, applying borders, and so on. However, it is always best to type the content first, and only then consider the presentation. There are a couple of reasons for this. First, it means that the content of the writing is done without excessive amounts of time being lost on formatting. Second, you might have noticed how 'glitches' sometimes appear on the page – points at which the formatting changes for no apparent reason. For instance, if you select a new font, the computer may drop back into the default font (usually Times New Roman). This can result in very strange changes of font within a document. Help your students avoid these glitches by using the 'Select All' function on the 'Edit' menu, and then choosing a new font and making other presentational changes after they have finished the work.

✓ *Save, save, save*: I'm sure that you too have had that awful experience where a student says 'My computer just froze/crashed and I lost all my work!' You can overcome this problem by insisting that your students name and save their documents right from the word go. When I am working with a whole class on computers, I spend the first ten minutes going around to check that everyone has named and saved their work. It is also a good idea to keep reminding your students to save their work every few minutes, as they write.

✓ *Use the 'ctrl' functions*: Microsoft Word offers the user a variety of shortcuts for the most commonly used functions, such as save, bold, italic and print. These shortcuts are, in my experience, largely ignored by students in favour of the pull-down menus at the top of the screen. However, these shortcut keys can save a great deal of time, particularly Ctrl+S for saving a document as you go along. (In fact, this should become an automatic reflex for them, every few minutes when writing on a computer.) These shortcuts are listed on the pull-down menus.

Writing and the interactive whiteboard

An interactive whiteboard (IWB) is essentially a 'live' computer desktop, but one that the teacher can scribble on, notate, interact with, and generally use as a tool for teaching. Although it's tempting to view your lovely IWB as automatically being a good thing in terms of learning, it's important to be aware of the potential downsides as well.

Research done thus far is split on whether IWBs automatically have a positive impact on student attainment. As with most things in the classroom, much depends on exactly how well the teacher uses them. However, the IWB is clearly a technology that will be in classrooms for the foreseeable future. Keep the potential downsides in mind, and take steps to mitigate or overcome them:

✘ You can present the class with lots of text without them seeing you actually doing any writing. Although you might annotate texts, there's a temptation to avoid much of the writing that you would have done on a plain old-fashioned whiteboard, by typing it up instead. A key part of modelling writing for your students is letting them view the 'teacher as writer': seeing you scribbling, thinking as you write, making mistakes, scrubbing them out. Make sure you do all these things on your IWB.

✘ There may be a tendency to focus on the technology rather than on the content and delivery of what you're actually teaching. Bear in mind that just because the presentation looks great, doesn't automatically mean the learning opportunities are great as well.

✘ The use of an IWB can lead to a teacher-directed style of learning – what used to be called 'chalk and talk'. The teacher retains control of the technology, and gets stuck at the front of the classroom next to the board. Remember to ensure that your students interact with the board as writers.

✗ There's also a tendency to use an IWB for whole-class teaching, because it is an efficient method for demonstrating activities to the class as a single group. This can mitigate against proper differentiation of the learning, for instance for the more able students.

✗ Using an IWB can slow down the pace of a lesson, particularly if the teacher is asking lots of low-ability students to come up and write ideas on the board.

To use your IWB to teach writing in the most effective way, you might use it to:

✓ show your class how to annotate a text – circling or underlining words, using different colours to highlight, and so on

✓ save the text, complete with annotations, to share with your students

✓ play video clips to inspire creative writing, or to provide research material for a non-fiction piece

✓ save materials for reuse and repetition, for instance with less-able students or for a student who has been absent

✓ brainstorm ideas as a class, for a specific writing task, although you must balance the need to maintain pace in your brainstorming with the advantages of getting the students up at the front writing down their ideas

✓ model different types of writing – presenting writing frames and filling in the details together with the class

✓ show your students how to assess and mark a piece of work, using marking symbols

✓ demonstrate how the marking criteria for an exam have been met (or not) within an essay

✓ give key vocabulary for a task being done in class

✓ play online interactive games to learn new techniques or skills

✓ focus in on a particular image or idea, by showing only one part of the screen

✓ show questions, and several possible answers

✓ move text around, for instance defining whether a word is an adverb or an adjective by moving it to the appropriate column

✓ use voting to see what the whole class thinks on an issue.

An IWB can be particularly helpful for those students who have special educational needs. The teacher can offer large fonts, colours, images, and so on to help them understand an activity.

Writing and the internet

We are still in the infancy of how we use the internet in education, and many teachers are still uncertain about what it offers us in terms of true educational value. There are so many different websites springing up (and going out of business) that it is very time-consuming to search for those that are actually worth a visit in terms of learning. When companies first started developing educational sites online, some tried a subscription-based model, with schools paying to access them. Although there are still some of these subscription sites around, there are also many free sites now available to the teacher.

When you're using the internet as a writing resource in your teaching, you might be:

✓ using it as a tool to research material for a piece of non-fiction writing
✓ finding inspiration for creative pieces, for instance using videos and images
✓ writing in forms that are found online, for example creating a website or using a social networking profile to examine a fictional character
✓ publishing your students' writing online, to celebrate their work.

When using the internet, remember:

✓ *There's no such thing as a free lunch*: Even free sites need to be funded in some way, in order to afford to run, and to produce good-quality content. There are sites out there that are not funded by advertising, but be aware that someone, somewhere is paying for the site to exist. Generally speaking, it works well to stick to the publicly funded sites, such as the BBC.
✓ *Be aware of advertising*: Be aware of the type and quantity of adverts to which your students are exposed. When planning a writing activity using the internet, check the sites first to find out how much advertising your students will see.
✓ *Find a good search engine*: A good-quality search engine will save you time and effort. It will also help you find relevant content for using in

specific curriculum areas. Google brings up good, clear results and is plain and straightforward to use.

✓ *Learn more about it*: There are some excellent books available to help you use the internet more effectively, and which give you information about the technical aspects of the worldwide web. For teachers who want to use the internet better in their classrooms, I recommend *The Internet in School* by Duncan Grey (Continuum, 2001), and *The Rough Guide to the Internet* by Peter Buckley and Duncan Clark (Rough Guides, 2009).

✓ Utilize your school website/virtual learning environment: Your school will have a website and probably also a virtual learning environment (VLE) of its own. Talk to the technology staff at your school to find ways in which you might utilize these to develop, track, assess and celebrate your students' writing.

As well as making the most of your own school's learning platform, a lot of teachers I meet recommend using Moodle – www.moodle.org. This e-learning platform allows you to create online courses of your own, to use with your students.

Creative ideas for using the internet

As well as using technology to help you deliver the learning, it can also be mined to find new forms and formats for writing. You could ask your students to:

✓ write an eBay listing, designed to persuade people to buy an unusual item ('My toenail clippings'), with a prize for the most persuasive piece

✓ write a Facebook page for a character in a book

✓ write a class website – I've used the free site www.weebly.com to set up several quick simple websites of my own.

Email and writing

The email is a very recent addition to the world of written communication. Not quite a letter, not quite a text message, the email is rapidly becoming a written form all of its own. There is quite a high level of informality in the email at present – we tend to use different vocabulary to that which we might use in a letter. The use of abbreviations (such as 'LOL') and 'emoticons' (such as ☺) is all part of this informality. In addition, correspondence between friends often does away with the need for 'proper' technique – punctuation, capital letters, paragraphing and so on.

There is much potential in the email for teachers interested in developing literacy. Here are a few ideas to get you started:

- ✓ *School/home communication*: Your school should provide you with a class email address. Use this to communicate with students and parents, for instance to send reminders about homework.
- ✓ *Chain stories*: Use email to create a 'chain story', with each recipient adding a sentence in turn, as they receive the message, and then sending it on.
- ✓ *Email and types of text*: Get your students to write emails for a variety of audiences and purposes: for instance, an email to a local paper protesting about the planned closure of a library.

Safety on the internet

One of the reasons why the internet is so wonderful for writing is that it can be used by anyone and everyone, as long as they have access to a computer. However, clearly this also has its disadvantages. When online, our students can communicate with other people very easily. It is all too easy for these people to pretend to be someone else, or to write abusive and bullying messages. We have all heard the horror stories of students being abused via contacts made on the internet.

Although schools now use filtering software, it is better to be safe than sorry, especially at this stage in the development of the technology. This is not a book on using the internet, nor is it a book about online safety. However, when using the internet as a writing resource, there are some important safety rules that you must reinforce with your students:

- – *Keep personal information personal*: Warn your students constantly about the dangers of giving out personal information on the internet, particularly if they are using chat-rooms. Tell them that they should never give out their age, telephone number or address under any circumstances. If they do use their real name, they should stick to using their first name only.
- – *Virtual people*: On the internet, we are 'virtual', we exist in cyberspace in the form that we choose to reveal. Get your students to think about how the people they communicate with via the internet could

be using a false persona. It is perfectly simple for a 50-year-old man to claim that he is a 15-year-old boy, with all the potential abuses that might result.

– *Never arrange meetings*: Because of this potential for dishonesty, make it clear to your students that they should never arrange meetings in person with the other users that they meet on the internet.

– *Safety settings*: The '10 per cent rule' applies to internet safety too. Make your students aware of how safety settings work (for instance making a social networking site private) and encourage them to actually use these settings.

– *Cyber-bulling*: Bullying has inevitably moved online: make it clear to your students that bullying via the internet is just as harmful and wrong as bullying in person.

– *Viruses*: Although we all know about computer viruses swishing around the net, there is still a real temptation to download material that could be infected. Perhaps opening an attachment that comes with an email, or downloading a picture or program. Explain to your students the potential damage that can be done when downloading material from the internet.

– *Access to adult sites*: Be fully aware that when your students use the internet, it is likely that some of them will try to access adult, or porn, sites. Even the best filtering software won't always prevent this from happening. Keep a close check on the kind of sites your students try to access.

– *Publishing content*: Students can be quite blasé about uploading, down-loading and using the content they find online. You'll need to ensure that they understand topics such as copyright, intellectual property and plagiarism. Explain to them how photos and videos they upload may be used and manipulated by others, in ways they had not wanted or expected.

Some useful websites for teaching your students about safety on the internet are www.thinkuknow.co.uk and www.digizen.org.

ICT: the practicalities

In this final section of the chapter, you will find advice on the practicalities of using ICT within the classroom. These ideas come from my own experiences of working with computers and technology within my own lessons.

Maximizing your ICT resources

The majority of schools now have a reasonable level of ICT resources. However, there will still be situations where a number of teachers are sharing a few computers between their classes, or where a class of 30 students will have to make do with one machine per pair or less. Here are some thoughts about how you can maximize your ICT resources, especially if they are limited:

✓ *Sharing computers*: This can be a recipe for disaster unless it is well managed by the teacher. When you do need your students to share computers, then the following advice will help.
  – Set the boundaries before work starts – this avoids time wasted on settling disputes.
  – Warn the students that they need to take it in turns to write, and specify how this will happen.
  – Allow each student ten minutes at a time, before swapping over.
  – Alternatively, divide the lesson time in half instead, for instance giving each student 30 minutes of an hour-long lesson.
  – Be aware that the student who is not 'hands on' at the computer must still have a sense of involvement in the task.
  – Alternatively, set a separate non-ICT task for those students who do not have access to a computer.

✓ *Reader and writer*: If your students are using the computer to type up work that has already been written down by hand, one of them can act as reader while the other types. Doing this helps develop other skills: the reader practises reading out loud, the writer has to work out how the words she hears are spelt.

✓ *Typing together*: If you feel that paired sharing of computers is not suitable for your students, you could ask them to type together. Depending on how slow they are, this might mean each student typing a word in turn, or perhaps a line or paragraph.

✓ *The computer as reward*: For many students ICT is a highly motivational activity, especially for those who do not have access to a computer at home. Make use of the fact that use of the computer is viewed so positively, and if you have limited access to machines, make them a 'reward' for those who behave or work well. Obviously, you still need to ensure curriculum entitlement for all. However, you will generally find that all your students want to earn this 'reward' and are willing to work hard to receive it.

✓ *Make it count*: If your access to ICT facilities is limited, make sure that the time you spend on computers really counts. Consider how

important the presentational aspects are, and whether it might be
more worthwhile to use the time to practise editing and building
pieces of writing.

✓ *Book well ahead*: There is nothing more frustrating than wanting to
use a computer room but finding it booked up for months ahead.
Your school or ICT department probably runs a booking system
for any computer rooms, and my advice would be to get in early
with your booking. Halfway into a term, when the teachers are
feeling like a few well-deserved lessons off, the computer room can
seem remarkably appealing and any free space will be quickly
snapped up!

✓ *Take care of the machines you do have*: With limited ICT resources, every
computer counts. Spend time teaching your students how to take
care of the machines – what to do if they crash, which parts are particularly fragile and should be handled with care, and so on. For
instance, the CD drive often takes a battering from negligent or poorly
behaved students. Insist that they treat the school machines as they
would a computer in their own home.

Potential computing hazards

The 'hazards' listed below range from the light-hearted to the potentially
serious, and all are problems I have experienced during my teaching
career. I must admit a certain admiration for the huge range of options
for mischief-making that my students have been able to dream up. Below
are some of the problems and suggestions for overcoming them.

✘ *Printout mania*: Many is the time that I have faced the problem of a
printer with a huge quantity of print jobs backed up on it, each one a
single page sent by the same student. This is the student who simply
refuses to believe that either (a) her work will eventually come out of
the printer, or (b) one copy of her work is sufficient. There are several
methods you could use to overcome this problem:
- Explain to your students that once they have sent a page to the
printer, it is stored in the printer's buffer memory. It will be
printed eventually, and definitely does not need to be sent time
and time again.
- Although it is useful to encourage your students to use the 'Ctrl'
functions as a shortcut, don't let them in on the secret of the 'Ctrl
P' function. Insist that they use the full process with the pull-
down menus when printing a document.

- Have a class rule that your students must ask permission before they send anything to print. If they refuse to go along with this, simply turn the printer off.

✗ *ClipArt crazy*: For students, there is apparently something magical about having pictures available to add into their work. This use of ClipArt can be problematic for a number of reasons:
  - Pictures often take a long time to send and print out. The consequent wait can lead to a whole class full of panicking students, sending the same pages to the printer over and over again, convinced that their work is not going to appear.
  - ClipArt pictures use up huge quantities of ink from the printer cartridge, thus making for a very high ink bill.
  - Time spent fiddling around with pictures, or searching through the picture library for a suitable image, is often time spent at the expense of the content of the written work.

✗ *Crashing computers*: Considering the amount of use (and often abuse) that school computers suffer, it is surprising that they don't crash more often than they do. However, a computer crashing before a student has saved his work can cause real difficulty and stress for the student and for the teacher.

✗ *Internet connection problems*: Think about possible connection problems when you plan to use the internet in your teaching. There is nothing more frustrating than planning a lesson based on visiting various websites, only to find that your students cannot access them. The level of difficulty will vary according to the way that your school actually accesses the internet, and how the network (if there is one) is set up.

✗ *Hidden windows*: Your students will be skilled at taking advantage of the function that allows the user to have various documents and programs open at the same time, in different 'windows'. If you open a document in Windows and then minimize it (a button with a single dash at the top right of the screen) you will notice that it 'hides' at the bottom. Keep an eye out for these hidden windows when your students are using computers. The devious amongst them may be logging into chat-rooms or onto their favourite websites when you are not looking, and then minimizing these as soon as they see you coming so that they can pretend to be working.

✗ *The disappearing mouse-ball*: If you have not yet experienced the disappearing mouse ball trick, then be aware that inside many types of mouse is a small ball, about the size of a gobstopper, which can be easily removed. Ask each student to turn his or her mouse upside down at the end of the lesson, so that you can check whether all the balls are still in place.

✗ *Swapping the keys*: When I encountered this one I was truly amazed: in fact I didn't know whether to laugh or to cry! Basically, it is not difficult to pull the keys away from the keyboard and then swap them about. The next person to use the computer will be thoroughly confused when their typing does not seem to be coming out as it should.

✗ *Fingers, fingers everywhere*: There is an attraction for some students, particularly the younger ones, in putting their fingers into every possible area of the computer. This is not only dangerous, but is also potentially damaging to the computer. If you experience this behaviour from your students, the simple answer is to ban them from using the machines until they can treat them with the respect they deserve.

✗ *The big freeze*: Spend some time explaining to your students what they should do if the computer crashes. The automatic reaction seems to be to turn the computer off at the mains, but if they do this the machine may be damaged. For those of you who do not already know, the best thing is to hit the Ctrl Alt and Delete buttons simultaneously, which will (almost always) reboot the computer. If that doesn't work, hold down the 'on/off' button for five seconds.

✗ *Safety on the internet*: I devoted a whole section to this issue earlier in this chapter, as it is now a really crucial issue for ICT use. Many of us are just beginning to see the classroom potential, both good and bad, that the internet offers. We need to develop an awareness of safety issues as soon as possible – after all, the students in our class are our responsibility. If we are going to introduce them to the world of the web, we need to ensure that they are properly equipped to deal with it.

Part 3

Everyone's a Writer

10

Supporting the Struggling Writer

It is not so much our friends' help that helps us, as the confidence of their help.

Epicurus

Our ultimate aim when teaching writing is to get all our students to learn to write, and preferably to learn to write well. If they don't succeed in this challenge, they will be disadvantaged for the rest of their lives. Those who are not fully literate are restricted in the type of employment they can find when they leave school. They are also limited in their ability to communicate via the written word, in a letter, an email or a job application. We owe it to all our students to develop their writing to the best of our (and their) ability.

This chapter focuses on how you can help your struggling writers: the less able, those with special needs, those to whom English is a second or additional language, and those whose behaviour has a negative impact on their progress in writing. Many of the strategies, approaches, activities and resources described in Chapter 1 will be highly beneficial for older students who are not yet writing well. Whatever approach you use, strive to balance your desire to get through the curriculum against your weak writers' need to gain confidence and retain self-esteem.

Where students struggle to express themselves, and to write well, school must feel hugely frustrating. Day after day the weak writer arrives at school, knowing full well that he must struggle to write in the majority of lessons. It is hardly surprising that weak writers tend to enjoy the practical subjects, such as PE, drama and art. At least in these areas they can communicate their ideas and complete the activities without having to write. When asked to write, a weak student will often lose his focus or resort to misbehaviour: embarrassed by his lack of skill and to hide his discomfort, he plays the 'class clown'.

Key strategies for the teacher

Happily there are plenty of approaches you can use to support those students who find writing a challenge equal to scaling Mount Everest. The following suggestions cover the teacher's attitude and expectations, and how he organizes the learning:

✓ *Don't believe the worst*: It is tempting to make negative judgements of your least-able students. The frustration of repeatedly being presented with poor pieces of writing makes you believe that these students are simply not putting any effort into their work. While this might be true for a minority, try to assume that your students try their hardest. At the same time, insist that they constantly strive to achieve better results. If there are students who present you with poor writing on a regular basis, ensure that they have been identified as possibly having learning difficulties.

✓ *Stay positive*: Try to retain a positive approach, looking for what has worked in the writing rather than focusing on what hasn't. It could be that your weakest writers have excellent and imaginative ideas, and it is merely the technique that prevents you from appreciating this. While I am not suggesting that you should praise poor work, be aware that these students face negativity and failure day after day, and that this cycle needs to be broken.

✓ *Watch your language*: Take care over what you say to your least-able children. When you are tired or stressed, it is all too easy to throw off a casual comment, such as 'This is terrible – you haven't made much effort with it, have you?' Remember that writing is an expression of who we are, and it is hard for writers of any age to accept criticism of their work. Aim to phrase your criticisms in a constructive way, identifying something that the student has done well, even if this is as simple as putting a title on the piece.

✓ *Use group activities*: For the least able, working as part of a group offers a welcome relief from the stress of individual writing. In a mixed-ability setting, the more-able students will often help their less-able counterparts to succeed. In addition, the least able can choose to complete those tasks that are best suited to their own talents, for instance drawing or design work.

✓ *Boost their confidence*: Find ways to boost the confidence of your weakest writers – to make them feel 'big' in the eyes of their peers. For instance, you might work with a small group to write a short poem, and then get them to present it to the rest of the class.

✓ *Take care with timings*: Give your weakest writers plenty of time to complete writing tasks, particularly when you're asking them to copy text off the board. When you set a homework task towards the end of the lesson, ensure that your weakest writers have been able to note it down. Alternatively, offer your weaker students a slip of paper with the homework written on it.

✓ *Consider seating positions*: Your weakest students may find it much easier to learn, work and focus if they are allowed to sit close to the board. This will help them write down ideas and activities; it will also minimize the chances of being distracted by the rest of the class.

Key strategies for the student

Just as there are useful ways of organizing your lessons, to support weaker writers, so there are strategies that focus on the student's experience of the learning. Make sure that you:

✓ *Use multi-sensory approaches*: Those students who have dyslexia, and those who prefer practical approaches, will really benefit from a multi-sensory approach to learning. For every activity, think about whether you can make it hands on, include images, and appeal to the whole range of senses. Use the kind of suggestions given in Chapter 1 to create multi-sensory writing activities for your students – bending pipe cleaners into words, tracing sandpaper letters with their fingers, and so on.

✓ *Set achievable targets*: Everyone needs something to strive for, but for the weak writer it may feel like there is so much that needs putting right that there is no point in even trying. Help your weak students develop their writing by setting small, achievable targets, and rewarding them when these targets are met. For instance, you might ask a student to aim for the neatest handwriting that she can produce, and reward her good efforts with a sticker. You could draw a line on the page, and ask the student to raise a hand when she reaches it, so you can go back and support her when she most needs it.

✓ *Give them a break*: Give your weakest writers a break from writing on occasions, especially those for whom the technical demands prove very stressful. This break might involve:
  – *The use of a scribe*: This could be the class teacher, a teaching assistant, or another student. Giving him a scribe to write down his ideas allows the student to focus on the content of his work, rather than worrying about technique.

- *The use of a recording device*: Talking into a recording device helps the student to develop oral skills, and to focus on developing the content of her work, without worrying about the need to spell, write neatly, and so on. After making the recording, the student could choose one part of her work to write out.
- *The use of a computer*: For students whose handwriting is very weak, using a computer gives a welcome break. If you have access to a portable computer, your least able writers might use this on a regular basis in the classroom.

✓ *Supply them with the tools they need*: Offer your weakest writers the tool kit they need to support them in their writing. While many teachers will write up a list of key words on the board, it's probably more useful to supply these words on small cards to your weaker writers. Being able to copy them up close is far easier than having to look between what they are writing and a board at the front of the room.

✓ *Identify common mistakes*: Work out which words your weak writers struggle with, and set activities for them to learn this vocabulary. Help them develop mnemonics that will really work for them. You can find a list of commonly misspelled words to use with more-able writers at the back of the book. Weak writers will tend to make mistakes on words that they cannot sound out to spell: any, many, does, doesn't, because, their, ought.

Key strategies for differentiation

Where you have a wide range of abilities in your class, you obviously want to differentiate the work as much as you can. What you're after is work that challenges your students, but at the same time feels achievable and gives them a sense of success. It can be tricky to find time to set a range of writing tasks in every lesson; it's also hard to manage a lesson where there are lots of different activities taking place. What often happens is the teacher differentiates 'by outcome', that is, by the fact that some students do well at an activity and others less well. But for those who do less well, a sense of failure can pervade.

There are plenty of other ways to differentiate – you could:

✓ *Adapt the task*: Make it simpler or shorter for your less-able students.
✓ *Set different targets*: Tell students, these are the targets you *must* achieve; try to complete these ones as well.

✓ *Use different timings*: Give more time to complete a task to your less able, with an extension activity for those who finish quickly.

✓ *Give additional resources*: Offer a bank of key words to your weaker writers, or give them a more detailed frame within which to work.

✓ *Use cloze procedure*: Cloze procedure, or 'fill in the blanks', is a great approach for weak writers. Essentially, you are offering a writing frame where nearly all the writing has already been done. To take this one step further, offer a bank of words at the bottom of the page, for the students to slot in.

✓ *Target support staff*: It's tempting to sit support staff with the less able. Take a range of approaches – sometimes, ask your teaching assistant to look after the rest of the class, while you sit and do focused work with your weak writers.

✓ *'Chunk back' activities*: Work out your ultimate aim for the work, for instance 'to write an essay'. Now work backwards, looking at the steps that a student must achieve in order to be able to fulfil this aim. Then figure where in these steps your weakest students are – can they paragraph/form sentences/sequence ideas?

Supporting students with English as a second or additional language

It is often very rewarding to teach students whose first language is not English: typically they are keen to learn, and they bring with them cultural and life experiences that differ from those of a typical student. These bi- or trilingual children have the advantage of being completely immersed in the English language during the course of the school day. Although this can mean they are slow to get going at first, eventually this immersion leads to a deeper knowledge of the new language.

When working with students who have English as a second or additional language, aim to:

✓ *Enhance grammatical understanding*: The difference between the structure of the mother tongue and of the English language often results in grammatical errors, for instance in the placement of verbs. Help students who have English as a second language (ESL) learn about word order and other areas of English grammar.

✓ *Develop grammatical awareness*: Help the individual student and the class as a whole by doing activities to develop grammatical awareness, for instance looking at the way regular verbs are conjugated in English.

185

✓ *Irregular verbs*: These are confusing for ESL students. Give them a list of how to conjugate the most commonly used irregular verbs, particularly 'to be'.

✓ *A two-way learning process*: Widen your own knowledge by asking an ESL student to teach you some words in his native language. This will make him feel special and help you in engaging your class.

✓ *Make the student an expert*: If the student is confident, ask him to share a few words of his language with the class: numbers from one to ten, the days of the week, different parts of the body. By sharing his expertise, the student gets to feel that he has an important contribution to make.

✓ *Give them key vocabulary:* Give the student with ESL a list of key terms or technical words in all the subjects of the curriculum. (Find these at the companion website.)

✓ *Give the student a translator*: If you have two students in your class who have the same mother tongue, but who are at different stages in their acquisition of English, ask one to act as a translator for the other.

✓ *Be aware of cultural differences*: Language divides us both in terms of communication, and also culturally. Aim to learn about and understand the cultures from which your students come, and how this might impact on their writing. For instance, the use of irony is prevalent in the English language, but not in some other cultures. Some students will be used to texts written in a way that we would consider to be 'back to front' – English texts will be doubly confusing to these students.

✓ *Work with texts from other countries*: Incorporate texts from other countries into your lessons. Show your ESL students that you value writing from all different cultures.

✓ *Find out about other countries*: Set projects on different countries as part of your class work. Ask the student or his parents to come and act as an 'expert', talking to the class about what their country of origin is like.

Writing and behaviour

For some students, writing is difficult because they cannot behave themselves: they lack concentration or get involved in low-level misbehaviour, such as chatting and leaving their seats. Below are some tips to help you get your students behaving properly, so that they can write to the best of their ability.

My key strategies include:

✓ *Set your boundaries*: When you set behaviour boundaries, make it clear how written work will take place. Make your boundaries sufficiently explicit from the start, so your students learn that this is the way they must work. Have boundaries both for behaviour during writing, and for the quality and quantity of work you expect to receive.

✓ *Be reasonable, but don't reason with them*: Some teachers like to set their boundaries in conjunction with the students, and this is fine. However, be clear that you are the one who sets the ultimate standards: who decides how learning takes place. Be reasonable about the standards you set – it's unrealistic to ask your class to work in silence for an hour. But if you ask for ten minutes silent writing, you do not need to debate whether this is OK or not with your students.

✓ *Explain your aims*: Set out the aims of the lesson clearly, to 'signpost' the learning that will take place. Do this at the start of each lesson, so that your students feel secure, and have a greater sense of purpose.

✓ *Always be polite*: Be polite in the way you interact with students, and in the way you react to their work. While it is tempting to be rude about writing that is of poor quality, this can be extremely destructive to students. Even if you are sure that poor work is a result of laziness, rather than weakness, you can still react politely and constructively. For instance, say 'I just know you can do much better than this' rather than 'This is an awful piece of writing.'

✓ *Set individual targets*: Targets are extremely useful for individual students who find writing difficult. Set high but realistic targets, and think about how many to give at any one time. It is better to set a single specific target, such as 'Put a full stop at the end of every sentence', rather than a generalized set of targets such as 'Get your punctuation and spelling right.'

✓ *Set whole-class targets*: When setting whole-class targets, divide the work up into:
  – the work that must be done
  – the work that should be done
  – and the work that could be done.
Your more able students can stretch themselves by aiming for all three targets; the less able retain a sense of achievement by completing the first two.

✓ *Use repetition*: Many times you explain a task only to find that, a few minutes later, several hands go up with students saying 'I don't understand what we're meant to do.' Use repetition when setting written work to clarify what must be done. After explaining the task, ask one of your students to repeat back to you the work that has been set.

✓ *Know when to be flexible*: At certain times of the day or week, or under certain conditions that are out of your control, your students may not be in the right mood to write. A class returning from a lively PE lesson may find it very hard to settle down to written work; on a wet Friday afternoon, your students might achieve little of value if they are asked to do an extended piece of writing. Know when to be flexible, and when practical work, speaking tasks or reading are more appropriate than writing.

✓ *Teaching styles*: For students with poor concentration, or in a class where there is a lot of misbehaviour, think carefully about suiting your teaching style to the students. You could:
  – begin the lesson with a fast-paced 'starter activity' or some music, to get poorly focused students in the mood for writing
  – start each lesson using a familiar pattern, to give a clear structure to the learning
  – avoid too much teaching from the front, especially with a class that tends to drift off-task
  – set short targets, and reward the completion of each part of the work
  – use activities that work for students with different learning styles, include plenty of active, hands-on work.

✓ *Developing focus*: To write well, you need to be able to focus on the task at hand. For students with poor concentration, who cannot stick at written tasks, use the focus exercises described in Chapter 4.

11

Extending the Gifted Writer

It is not enough to have a good mind; the main thing is to use it well.

Rene Descartes

At the opposite end of the spectrum from the least able are your really able, or gifted, students. These students have the potential to become, or indeed already are, exceptionally skilled writers. It is tricky to plan in challenges for those at the top end of the ability range in a mixed-ability classroom, while still giving the opportunity for the less able to succeed. Even if your class is set by ability, there will still be a wide range of different levels within the traditional 'top set'. You can find some key strategies for differentiation in Chapter 10. This chapter gives advice on the kind of extension activities you might use within lessons, to stretch your most able.

Challenging starters

The start of a lesson is a great point at which to challenge the thinking of your most able students. Use starters that are engaging, and which can be accessed and completed at different levels, including the use of higher-order thinking skills. For instance:

✓ *A mystery* – 'There's been a murder!' – Use the crime scene detailed on p. 200 to get your students really engaged and curious.
✓ *A surprise* – 'Say the colour' – This activity demonstrates the clash between left-brain and right-brain thinking – the student is asked to say the colour a word is written in, rather than the word itself. Find a worksheet to use with your class at the companion website.
✓ *A challenge* – Use the classic '10 uses for ...' activity to stimulate your students' thinking. When you say 'go', the students work in groups to come up with *at least 10*, and preferably 20, uses for a simple object. There is no 'right or wrong', and their ideas can be as crazy, weird, unusual or silly as they like. Your object could be:

- a paper clip
- a plastic bottle
- a piece of string
- a carrier bag.

Structuring the learning

Consider the way that you structure and format your lessons and writing activities, so that you stretch the most able. Here are some thoughts about how you might achieve this:

✓ Vary the patterns – does everyone do the same in this lesson, or are there different options on offer?
✓ Who makes the choice about which activities to complete – can you offer the students an element of choice in this?
✓ The use of 'learning stations' works well when offering choice to a class – have several activities on offer, and move the students around or set them targets of what you wish them to complete.
✓ Enable your students to access different resources – sets of key words, props, a variety of texts to inspire them.
✓ Involve your students in planning their own learning – what do they want or need to learn?
✓ Encourage your most able students to come up to the front to teach the others.
✓ When planning, consider the extension tasks that might work well for a topic, rather than coming up with these on the spot.
✓ Set homework, such as projects, which can be completed at a variety of levels.

Finding a 'voice'

One of the aspects that sets your gifted writers apart from the rest is that they are developing their own 'voice'. Each piece of writing they produce 'sounds like' them, no matter what form it takes. This is one of the most complex aspects of being a writer: finding your own 'voice' and maintaining it so that it shines through, whatever you're writing.

When you find your own voice, you create a connection with an audience of readers that goes beyond the content of what you've written. The reader feels a sense that they somehow know you, even though you've never met. Think of your own favourite writers – a novelist, perhaps, or a newspaper columnist. Something about their voice chimes with you and makes you want to read what they say.

Finding a 'voice' is essentially about studying and understanding style. Give your students plenty of texts to work with. Use the 'Studying style checklist' which you can download at the companion website.

Developing a writing style

Here are some activities and approaches to use with your most able, to help them develop a style of their own:

✓ *Learn to listen to the 'voice'*: Encourage your able students to hear their voice internally as they work, listening to the writing in their head, simultaneously reading and writing. Encourage them to bring out their own personality within the writing: if they have a good sense of humour, this might mean adding splashes of humour or informality, if they have strong opinions; they could adapt the way that they use punctuation and italics to give emphasis.

✓ *Echo other strong voices*: A great way to develop your own voice as a writer is to practise 'echoing' the voice that other writers use. When looking for suitable texts, pick writers who have a strongly identifiable voice of their own: for instance, writing a detective story 'in the style of' Elmore Leonard or Raymond Chandler.

✓ *Use rewriting activities*: Another useful exercise for able students is to rewrite the work of other authors in a different style. This might mean reworking a broadsheet newspaper article into the style of a tabloid; turning an adult story into one for children; or changing a formal letter into an informal one. As your students do this, they learn to adapt the vocabulary, timing, sentence length, style, etc. as appropriate.

✓ *Use analysis activities*: Get your able students to analyse the way that other writers work. They can then adapt and apply this knowledge to their own writing. For instance, they might look at how writers in different genres structure their sentences to create a sense of pace and rhythm, and to develop tension. They could look for the use of language devices within a text and consider the effects that these create. The best writers are often the most avid readers, and your talented students are probably subconsciously analysing the books that they read already.

✓ *Develop linguistic techniques*: Able students should be capable, from a very young age, of using imagery and other linguistic techniques in their work. Don't be afraid to introduce these techniques to your class earlier than the curriculum suggests. Encourage your able students to use techniques such as repetition, extended metaphors and alliteration in subjects right across the curriculum.

✓ *Develop the use of punctuation*: Encourage your very able students to explore a more advanced use of punctuation. For instance, teach them when it is appropriate to use a colon or semi-colon, and the syntactical rules behind this. Again they can learn to do this ahead of the rest of the year group.

✓ *Break the rules*: Students who are very able writers may need to learn how to bend the rules once in a while. The 'best' writers are not merely technically accurate, but also have imagination and a willingness to experiment. The more conscious this bending of the rules is, the better it works. It's not about making mistakes, but about a writer who has complete control of his writing style. For instance, your students might play with grammar to create a sense of personal style, splitting infinitives or writing incomplete sentences.

✓ *Develop vocabulary*: Make sure that your most able writers have access to a thesaurus and a dictionary. Encourage them to widen their vocabulary, and to consider a range of words, picking out the one that is most appropriate to the context and sound of what they are writing. Ask them to explore the definition of unfamiliar words, using a dictionary to consider the subtle variations of meaning that are available.

✓ *Think about sound*: The best writers consider the sound of the words that they use, as well as their meaning. Encourage your students to consider the way that their language sounds by reading it out loud to others – either in the class or at home.

✓ *Encourage a sense of self*: As well as having their own voice, good writers put a sense of themselves into their work. This might mean offering an emotional response to a subject, or referring to personal experiences to back up the point being made.

✓ *Encourage inter-textual reference*: As their work becomes more complex, able writers should be encouraged to look for other texts to refer to in their writing. Inter-textual reference might involve quoting an acknowledged expert on a subject, or it could mean referring to a link that they have discovered between one novel or author and another.

Essay writing with the most able

Writing essays is an excellent way to stretch the writing skills of your most-able students. Through the medium of an essay, these students might explore different ways of structuring their work, or look at using linguistic techniques to give their writing more interest. Here are some strategies for working on essay-writing with your strongest students.

✓ *Develop the use of tone*: The best essays use a writing style that reflects the tone of their subject. If a student is writing about a piece of text with a sad, emotional theme, this could be reflected in the choice of words and style of the essay. Get the student to go through her essay with a highlighter, picking out the words that are there mainly to create tone, rather than to convey meaning.

✓ *Develop the use of language devices*: Language devices can be used within essays in any subject area. For instance, the writer might use repetition to link together a series of ideas over several paragraphs. He could use a metaphor to deepen an explanation or alliteration to make the writing sound more appealing. He might use the technique of 'listing in threes', with three points listed in turn, building in power and emphasis each time.

✓ *Develop the use of pace*: Pacing a piece of writing is a subtle skill. Your most able students could experiment with altering word or sentence length, and adding or taking away punctuation, to vary the pace of the writing within an essay.

✓ *Develop a 'voice'*: The best essays give the reader a sense of the writer's 'voice'. A satirical essayist might use a cynical tone, a more emotional essay-writer could use a passionate voice. Maintaining a consistent 'voice' throughout an essay will make the writing far more appealing to the reader.

✓ *Give the reader something to chew on*: An essay that includes a surprise fact or comment, or that concludes by leaving a question hanging in the air, can be very powerful. Encourage the most polished essay writers amongst your students to make their essays striking for the reader.

Perhaps the main issue to watch with very able students, is that they don't overdo their writing. Encourage them to read, review and edit their work and put a focus on clarity and simplicity, as well as on clever use of language.

12

Boys and Writing

Of all the animals, the boy is the most unmanageable.

Plato

When it comes to writing, there's a definite gap between the levels that boys and girls achieve in their assessments in schools. Many teachers (of literacy at primary level, or English in secondary schools) feel this instinctively; there's also lots of data and research to back this up. There has been much debate over the years about why boys are less successful in their writing at school than girls. This is a book of practical ideas and strategies for teaching writing, rather than a theoretical analysis of why such a gender gap exists. However, on a practical level it is worth asking yourself:

- Are my ideas of what 'good' writing looks like influenced by my gender?
- Do I have different expectations of how boys will or should work and behave in English or literacy lessons?
- Are the tasks I set more likely to appeal to one particular gender?
- Do I avoid setting certain tasks for fear of being seen to stereotype children by their gender?
- Does the working environment in my classroom mean that one group is more likely to be successful than the other?
- Does the gender of the literacy/English teachers at my school have an influence on children's/adults' perceptions of the subject?
- Does the way that our educational system is set up (including exams, formal learning and the curriculum) mitigate against boys' success in writing?

In the politically correct world of education, it is tricky for teachers to stand up and say 'I've noticed that this approach works best with my boys or (indeed) with my girls.' However, for the benefit of this chapter, I'd like to ask that you forgive any stereotyping or sweeping generalizations. The ideas you'll find here are simply practical suggestions about things that have worked for me (and for other teachers I know) in developing their boys' writing. I'm not suggesting that these should be the only approaches that you use, or indeed that you should pander to what your boys want all the time. However, where getting writing from your students is a struggle, where you have a class of mainly boys, or where you simply want to try something different, these approaches will help you succeed.

Expectations of boys' writing

First, challenge your own expectations of what makes 'good' writing. Don't always base your opinion on the latest target descriptors, or curriculum focus, or whatever the government 'hot topic' is at that moment. You're a reader – you have your own opinion about what a good book (or news report, or film script) looks and sounds like. Similarly, others will have a *different* opinion. Maybe you love romance books, chick lit, crime fiction, science fiction, horror or the classics? Perhaps you never pick up a novel, but devour a wide range of newspapers? There are examples of good writing in every single genre, but we don't all like or read them equally.

In our urge to get the best results possible with the class, it's tempting to teach students to write 'by the book' – to give them a kind of formula of 'what to include'. But good writing is not actually about stuffing as many connective words and descriptive phrases into a piece as you can (typically, something at which girls excel). Nor is it necessarily about the length of a piece or its presentation (again, often areas where girls are at their best). It's worth considering that, asked to name the ten most influential writers of the last millennium, many people would produce a list including mostly male writers.

When looking at how 'good' boys' writing is, make sure that you:

✓ *Consider quality versus quantity*: Boys often turn out shorter pieces of writing than their female classmates. There's a natural tendency for us to make a judgement based on quantity as well as quality. However, the best and most effective pieces of writing are often very concise. When marking and assessing work, consider whether the boys in your class actually achieve as much as the girls, but are simply doing it with less words.

✓ *Consider presentation versus content*: Similarly, you might find that your male students do not present their work in as attractive a way as their female counterparts. Their writing can be scrappy, and there are rarely any neatly coloured pictures accompanying their work. Again, remember to focus on the quality of the content rather than allowing the appearance of the writing to sway your judgement.

✓ *Aim to be gender-neutral*: Overall, within the teaching profession, there are far more female than male teachers. The vast majority of primary school teachers are female, and this inevitably has an influence on boys during their primary years, while they are first acquiring literacy skills. Men and women tend to have different priorities in their reading interests, and in what they view as 'good' writing. When you read and mark your students' work try your hardest to judge it from a 'gender-neutral' position.

An interesting exercise is to mark a piece of work that your students have typed up, without knowing the name or gender of the students when you mark it. Can you 'spot' a male/female piece of writing?

Motivating boys to write

Making your students write is not all that difficult – you simply offer an incentive for doing it, and a consequence for not. Making them *want* to write, on the other hand, is often very tricky indeed. This is particularly so for those boys who have struggled with literacy throughout their school career. By the time they get to your bottom set GCSE class, they will have been failing to succeed at writing for over a decade. No wonder they get put off and feel disaffected.

Often, when boys are inspired by or engaged with something, it becomes an interest to the point of obsession. You can harness this intense focus to encourage your boys to do more writing, both in the classroom and beyond. Typically, your male students will be genuinely motivated to write when one or more of the following statements is true:

✓ It's about something that really interests me.
✓ I can definitely see the point of doing it.
✓ It will help me achieve a key goal.
✓ I want to know how it works – how it's put together or how it comes apart.
✓ I'm finding out lots of fascinating information here.
✓ It's real, rather than made up.
✓ I'm going to win something by doing it.

✓ I can prove that I'm the best at this.
✓ If I follow these simple steps I can achieve a good end result.
✓ It makes me laugh.
✓ It's totally disgusting!

Of course, there may be a conflict between the learning that would best motivate your boys, and what the curriculum requires you to do. I've always believed that teachers should have the guts to say 'Stuff the curriculum' where they know that a particular task or text simply won't work with a particular group of students in the way that it's 'meant' to be taught. You have a choice: you can force them to slog through an activity, knowing full well that they will either misbehave, or alternatively do it so badly that it is hardly worth doing, or you can trust your professional instincts and reinvent the task or text so that it does actually engage them. 'Are they actually going to learn from doing this?' is a key question to keep asking yourself.

It's a case of thinking creatively – of moulding the bit of the curriculum or the skills you have to teach, to ensure that you get genuine motivation from your boys whenever possible. You'll find lots of ideas about how to do exactly that in the sections that follow. Here's one example of how I've done this in my own classroom.

For example: Songs as poems

I was teaching a low-ability GCSE English group, consisting mainly of boys. The behaviour of the group was just about OK; it was the disaffection with the subject that was tricky to handle. They just didn't want to write – they didn't see the point of it, it had no relevance to their lives. I could threaten all manner of sanctions, or offer all kinds of rewards, but they didn't care enough for it to make any difference. I needed to teach them some poetry analysis techniques, but the idea of presenting them with 'proper' poems seemed downright foolish.

What I did know was that these lads were really into their music – quite a lot of them would spend break times in the school's music studio. We had talked previously about their favourite bands. It occurred to me that song lyrics are a kind of poetry. So, here's the activity I did with them.

✓ Get hold of a selection of different song lyrics.

✓ Choose lyrics that relate to more traditional poetry in some way – they might rhyme, or have interesting metaphors, or have a particular rhythm.

✓ Present them to the class set out as 'poems'.

✓ Read out one of the 'poems' with the class – see if anyone spots what you've done!

✓ Now play the music/song to the class.

✓ Analyse tone, emotion, metaphor and so on – how does the kind of music relate to the words?

✓ You can follow this activity up by thinking about what music might provide a good match to some set poems – there's a useful link to 'tone' here.

Seeing that poetry was so closely connected to the music they loved so much was a great way to inspire my class. A particularly popular simile was 'like a bat out of hell'! Later, we moved on to look at how similar techniques were used in what they called 'proper, old fashioned' poetry.

Inspirational topics for boys' writing

There are particular genres that seem to appeal strongly to the majority of boys, and the wise teacher finds a way to capitalize on their interests. These genres include specific types of fiction, but they also include particular forms of writing. As well as thinking about using these genres to inspire writing, encourage your boys to read widely within these genres as well: the more widely they read, the better their writing will be. With reluctant older readers, offer them a book of short stories, or even a comic or magazine.

Many boys prefer to read non-fiction texts rather than stories. Remember that you can use a fictional genre (crime, science fiction) to inspire non-fiction writing. Similarly, you can use a non-fiction format (crime scene report, captain's log) to inspire a fictional piece. The following list includes just some of the genres and themes that inspire boys of all different ages, followed by a couple of examples of how these genres and themes could be used in your classroom.

- ✓ fables and myths
- ✓ mythical creatures
- ✓ fantasy
- ✓ horror
- ✓ monsters
- ✓ robots
- ✓ aliens
- ✓ science fiction
- ✓ magic
- ✓ superheroes
- ✓ pirates
- ✓ crime and murder mystery
- ✓ action, thrillers
- ✓ dangerous animals – lions, tigers, bears
- ✓ volcanoes
- ✓ computers/computer games
- ✓ football and footballers
- ✓ music
- ✓ rap
- ✓ toilet humour
- ✓ slugs, snails, yucky creatures
- ✓ wrestling, fighting

For example: The football team

This project came about when I was working with a very low-ability Year 8 group. Again, the class was mostly boys: literacy levels were weak, behaviour was awful! In most lessons, I was getting maybe a handful of words or a couple of sentences at most. Deciding that I had to find a theme that would inspire them, I came up with the idea of them being managers of either a pop group or a football team. Perhaps unsurprisingly, most of the boys chose to manage a football team.

Divide your students into groups of about four or five, and then give them a long list of challenges to complete. The tasks could include:

- ✓ Choose a name for your team.
- ✓ Design and label a kit for your team (home and away).

✓ Design, name and label a stadium for your team.
✓ Create and print a programme for a match.

For the full list of tasks, in a version that you can download and photocopy to use with your class, visit the companion website. You might like to specify particular roles within the group, or let the students give out the jobs themselves.

By the second lesson on this project, the boys were coming in with armfuls of old football programmes and football magazines, to use for research. They were so engaged that I was finally freed up to go round and sit with individuals and groups, and work on their writing skills.

For example: The scene of the crime

This idea has been a firm favourite of mine for many years. It works well as a drama project, but it's equally useful in an English lesson. I've found it fantastic for engaging the boys, and for getting them to write and express themselves in a variety of formats. I originally devised the lesson to try and engage a tricky group of Year 9 boys. It worked a treat!

✓ Set up a 'crime scene' in the corner of the classroom, with lots of interesting props. I usually set up some kind of card game, with money, drinks, fake blood, etc.
✓ If possible, it's great if you can use real crime scene tape to cordon the area off – this adds that vital touch of realism so beloved of students. You can buy crime scene tape online – see the companion website for suppliers.
✓ Bring your class into the room and explain to them that they are going to work as 'police detectives' to solve a crime.
✓ Nominate a 'chief of police' – this student will show the various bits of evidence to the class and encourage them to ask questions about what they observe in the crime scene.
✓ Get the students to complete a 'police report' form. This is basically just a writing frame on which your students can write their observations.

Go to the companion website to download my version of a 'Police report', which you can photocopy to use with your class as a frame for their writing. You can then move on to do witness interviews, to reconstruct the crime, to write news reports about what happened – take the theme in whatever direction you wish, really.

You can adapt this approach so that it also works when you're studying a text involving a crime. I've used this to do work on *Romeo and Juliet*, starting with the 'crime scene' at the end of the play and working backwards. I've also used this approach for a GCSE group who were studying the Arthur Miller play *A View from the Bridge*. We worked our way right up to a trial scene, with judge, defence, prosecution and jury!

Teaching techniques to inspire boys

Just as certain genres will appeal to your boys, so you can adapt the way you create activities so that boys find them more attractive. This might mean using a specific approach, structuring the work in a certain way, or applying a particular teaching technique.

Structuring activities
Boys work best when you:

✓ use a series of short tasks, rather than one longer one – two minutes, three minutes, five or ten at most
✓ set clear time targets before the activity begins – I like to use 'when I say go' to give a sense of pace and momentum to a task
✓ are specific about what you want them to achieve – 20 words, ten ideas, three full sentences properly punctuated
✓ find activities that *mean* something – that have a clear purpose and seem 'real' to your boys
✓ look for tasks that are topical, with links to something happening in the real world (this could be news-related or a career you know your boys would like to pursue)
✓ use activities that relate to a particular interest or hobby that your boys have outside school
✓ have an element of competition, for instance pitting one group against another, or seeing who can find the most ideas in a short time

✓ push them to find the limits – the most terrifying monster, the longest list of alliterative words, the worst poem or shortest story ever written.

Useful approaches for boys

Boys seem to love:

✓ Finding out how things work – picking something apart and putting it back together again. This approach works with a car engine, but it can equally apply to language – deconstructing sentences, looking for patterns in language, analysing a longer text to see how many pages are in each chapter, and so on.

✓ Using 'difficult' technical terms that in theory might be above the age or ability level of the class. For instance, a term such as 'pathetic fallacy' sounds grand, but is actually fairly straightforward to understand and easy to demonstrate (try taking your students outside in the lashing rain).

✓ Gathering ideas and information in a slightly 'off the wall' manner, for instance via Post-it notes, or on large sheets of paper on the floor.

✓ Active and interactive approaches – finding content for their writing in an active, rather than a passive, way. For instance, taking a trek around the school with clipboards to collect short snippets of overheard dialogue.

✓ Being asked to write short, tight and concise pieces, rather than longer, descriptive ones.

✓ Plenty of non-fiction activities; fictional texts approached using non-fiction formats.

✓ An element of choice in how they might present their work.

✓ Working together in a group to achieve an end result (for instance, as in my 'football managers' project).

✓ Being given writing activities that involve action, rather than description.

✓ Activities that prick their curiosity – a mystery to solve, a puzzle to work out.

For example: Dramatic attention!

I was exploring the notion of how language can be used to create suspense and dramatic tension with a Year 10 class, by analysing short stories. I set the students the task of working out how suspense and dramatic tension are created – what specific words or techniques did this within the story we were studying? They then had to devise a graph to show the exact levels of tension at key points in the story. Each 'high point' had to be accompanied by a quote from the story. The students had to explain exactly why this quote created tension (short sentences, scary vocabulary and so on). Afterwards, we wrote our own short stories full of dramatic tension.

✓ Analysing language to figure out how it works, and presenting the information they find in a graphic way. See above for an example.

Engaging formats for boys' writing

Boys enjoy certain formats more than others, and these will typically include:

✓ story maps – visual interpretations of a story, to show how plot and storyline work
✓ sequencing – for instance, with a washing line and pegs, sequence key events from a story
✓ speaking and listening-based activities – recording interviews is a particular favourite
✓ role play and drama – writing from *within* a character (for older students, choose 'characters' from real life – detective, chief executive, prime minister)
✓ using ICT to present their writing
✓ films and visual imagery
✓ photo stories – getting hands-on with a digital or video camera is a great way to engage your boys
✓ anything involving even a hint of a relationship to computer games, which are great for activities involving sequenced narratives and retelling stories
✓ comic strips and graphic texts
✓ scripting and making animations or cartoons
✓ sound effects and sound tracking
✓ magazines – cutting out sections from magazines, rewriting items, producing a magazine of their own for a real audience

✓ media-based approaches – writing and then videoing scripts
✓ basing their writing on films or television shows with which they're familiar
✓ visualizing a movie and then writing it from the camera's viewpoint.

As well as thinking about engaging topics for your boys, and the kind of forms in which they like to write, you can also experiment with getting them writing in unusual places. You'll find that this approach is engaging for your girls, as well as for your boys.

You might get your class to write on clipboards, in an area of the school grounds, or in a 'den' under the desks in your classroom, built using sheets, materials and tables. You could also use a wooded area if you have one, around a camp fire, in the style of Gareth Malone.

Part 4

Writing it Right

13

Writing and Assessment

You can't fatten a pig by weighing it.

> *Traditional saying*

Much of the writing that our students do at school is assessed, whether it is marking their exercise books, keeping a record of work to assess their progress in class, or writing for externally assessed examinations. However, we should never consider that our students are writing *for* assessment – the writing must always have a reason, and an audience, beyond this. This chapter gives ideas about the most effective ways for teachers to approach assessment, in terms of the potential for learning. I also look at how we can help our students deal with writing and its assessment in public exams.

Increasingly, it seems, teachers are being asked to assess, grade and keep evidence of students' writing from a very early age. Whilst this is not the place for a discussion of the rights and wrongs of this approach, constant testing can erode the self-esteem of those who most need help. As you mark and assess your students' writing, maintain a constant awareness of the effect on your poorly motivated students, those with special needs and the least able. Balance the potential damage done against the potential gain in terms of learning: trust your professional judgement to make the right choices.

Please note that this chapter is not about the latest government strategy for the assessment of writing, whatever that might be at the moment when you read this book. Instead, it is about approaches to the assessment of writing that will help your students become better writers, rather than about tracking how much of an improvement they have made. Or, to put it another way, this chapter is about ideas for getting your pigs to put on weight, rather than working out how fat they have become.

Assessing writing

If you ask the students in your class to explain *why* you mark their writing, what would they say? Do they see it as an exercise where the teacher finds out what they have done right or wrong, and how good their writing is? Or do they see it one of a range of strategies you use to help them understand what is effective in their writing, and to learn how to improve their own writing by and for themselves?

When we mark a piece of writing, we make a judgement, acting as both reader and reviewer of what the student has produced. This is a very powerful position, and making judgements on someone else's writing needs to be done with care and sensitivity. Writing is such a personal thing, such a reflection of our own personalities. Our ultimate aim should be for our students to play both roles – to be able to read, review and edit their own work, until they are happy with the end result and ready to show it to an audience if they wish.

When marking, keep constantly in mind the purpose of the assessment: what you are actually marking *for*. Is it to help the student improve expression or use technique better? Is it mainly about helping him develop the content of the work? Is it to see where students are in relation to each other, to assist with planning for future learning? In all circumstances, the assessment should be *for the student's learning*, and not just so that there is something to go in a mark book.

It is fair to say that at times, when teachers are overburdened with paperwork or the myriad pressures of the job, marking becomes little more than a paper exercise. It's a job that needs to be done, but there's little time to think about the reasons behind it and its potential benefits. Don't beat yourself up when this is the case – sometimes good enough has to be good enough.

It's worth reminding yourself, though, to keep in mind the best motivation for marking – to help your students learn what is good and bad about their written work, and how they might improve it. Here are just some of the different ways in which marking can help in this learning process:

✓ showing the child where he has made errors
✓ helping him to understand why he has made these mistakes
✓ helping him understand how to avoid making the same mistakes again
✓ showing him what is good or effective about his work
✓ helping him learn why these particular aspects of his writing are effective

✓ helping him to repeat the effective parts of what he has written
✓ helping him understand how to develop those ideas or techniques further
✓ making the student feel positive about his written work, to motivate him
✓ praising the student for what has gone well, to encourage him in the future
✓ setting targets for the future
✓ explaining how to reach these targets.

Top tips for assessment

There's never enough time in teaching, and so it pays to use the time you do have to its best advantage. The following strategies, ideas and techniques will help your students get the most out of the marking you do:

✓ Be clear about what you're looking for – talk through the objectives of the activity before your students start to write. What will a successful piece of writing look like?
✓ Refer back to those objectives in your marking – both those your students have achieved and those that they haven't.
✓ Where students haven't met the objectives, don't rule out other achievements for praise – things that were 'outside the box' of the original activity set.
✓ Use a highlighter to identify the points in the writing where the student has achieved a particular objective.
✓ Give 'improvement prompts', either in the form of statements ('You've used a lovely simile here') or questions ('Could you develop this idea further?' 'What is the character thinking at this point?').
✓ Mark writing as quickly as possible after it has been done – preferably while it's still fresh in the student's mind.
✓ Balance constructive criticism with targeted praise: use your knowledge of your students to work out what will be best for them.
✓ Give your students time to actually read your comments. Plan this in as an integral part of the lesson.
✓ Consider having a 'focus group' whose writing you will mark in detail on a particular task, particularly in the upper primary age range.

At the same time, give your students plenty of chances to write without the pressure of being marked. Be brave enough to let them throw their writing away, rather than feeling the need to keep evidence of every single piece of writing they ever do.

Marking symbols

Marking the technical aspects of a piece of writing takes a surprisingly long time, especially if you write out corrections in full. This is where marking symbols come in handy, helping make the job of marking much faster and more efficient. Sharing these symbols with our students should also enable them to correct their own drafts more quickly and effectively.

You can find some of the more commonly used symbols in Appendix 4 and as a downloadable resource at the companion website. An excellent way of encouraging your students to use and understand these symbols is to photocopy them to go in the front of student exercise books. Spend some time going through their meanings with your class, and practise using them on a piece of work. Even the youngest writers will be able to understand and use at least some of these symbols.

Marking methods

Marking comes in many forms: from the helpful to the destructive, from the specific to the generalized. Detailed marking can be incredibly time-consuming, and it is vital for the teacher to make some decisions about what will be marked, and in how much detail. It's a balancing act – you just cannot, as a working teacher, mark every single piece of work in full detail. Below are some thoughts on the different systems of marking that you might use, and some comments on the advantages and disadvantages of each method.

✓ *Close marking*: Many people (including parents, managers and inspectors) view this as the ideal form of marking. With this style of marking, each and every error is identified, and detailed comments are made on how the student can improve her work. Close marking has its drawbacks. It is very time-consuming for the teacher. It can be offputting (and potentially damaging) for students to receive back their writing completely covered in the teacher's pen. In addition, students will probably just skim over a page with masses of corrections on it. On the plus side, close marking can be useful in helping older and very able students to develop complex pieces of writing such as essays.

✓ *Tick and flick*: This type of marking involves placing a big tick (or cross) at the end of each question, paragraph or page, then turning (or 'flicking') to the next. A brief comment may be made at the end of the piece of writing. Although the teacher can say he has 'marked' the work, this method is not effective when it comes to the students learning from their mistakes. However, they do like their work to look 'marked', and the teacher gains a sense of how well they are doing and which areas need further work.

✓ *Marking for specific errors or features*: With this type of marking, the teacher identifies an area of concern, or a feature on which he would like the students to concentrate, before the writing takes place. The students are clear about the learning goal or objective, whether that is technical ('focus on getting your punctuation correct') or based on a skill or technique ('use an extended metaphor in this piece'). The teacher then looks specifically at these aspects as he marks the work.

✓ *Mark and amend/Mark and respond*: With this method, the teacher does some close marking, and asks the students to play an active role in responding to the marking that has been done. This make be in the form of answers to some questions he's posed at the end of a piece. It could be that they get into the habit of writing out spelling mistakes correctly, three times, in the back of their books.

Of course, the majority of us employ marking strategies that fall somewhere in the middle of all the above, depending on the amount of time that we can afford to give to marking the work. It is useful sometimes to step back and consider how the marking that you do actually impacts on the quality of your students' learning. Although 'ticking and flicking' might make their books 'look' marked, how much good is this form of marking actually doing? If you tend to focus more on 'close' marking, consider whether your students might feel that this implies a criticism of their writing, and whether it might demotivate them.

Strategies for assessment

Given the time-consuming nature of marking, it is important to consider strategies for making the job more effective and less time-intensive. It is tempting to see marking as something that the teacher does for the students, but this should not always be the case. In fact, some of the best learning can come from employing more unusual approaches. Here are some ideas for you to try, which will also save some of your valuable time. These approaches can be used in conjunction with the teacher's marking and assessment.

✓ *Marking each other's work*: Ask your students to swap over their writing, and to make evaluative comments on their classmates' work. Typically, students enjoy the chance to 'be teacher'. This strategy can help motivate your students, as it shows them what others within their peer group are achieving. Looking at other people's work (whether 'good' or 'bad') is vital for an understanding of what constitutes effective writing.

✓ *Marking the work together*: There are many opportunities for written work to be marked as a whole-class activity, especially where there are definitive right answers, for instance with spelling tests. The teacher gives the answers while the students tick or cross each one and put a mark or grade at the end. The students could mark their own work (if you trust them) or they could swap over and mark somebody else's.

✓ *Marking across peer groups*: An interesting alternative, especially for the secondary teacher with several teaching groups, is to ask your older students to mark the work of their younger counterparts, and vice versa. This is particularly useful where you have a class under-achieving (for instance, in Year 9) and another group with high levels of achievement (for example, in Year 7). The embarrassment of marking work that is actually better than theirs, although done by younger students, should make them buck up their ideas.

✓ *Marking 'created' work*: As well as using other students' work, do some writing yourself to create pieces that make exactly the point you had wanted. For instance, you might do a piece of writing with specific punctuation errors in it, and ask your students to go through it and use marking symbols to put it right.

To my mind, one of the key strategies you should use is to have high standards in relation to what you believe the student can do. Use your knowledge of each individual to pitch the learning at the right standard.

Effective questioning techniques

High-quality assessment is about knowing the right kind of questions to ask your students, in relation to their own writing, and to the writing of others. Effective questioning is about using open-ended questions that encourage higher-level thinking, rather than closed questions which have only one answer.

Here are some suggestions about the kind of questions you could include in your marking and discussion activities:

✓ How did you know that?
✓ How can you work out whether ...?
✓ How can we be sure that ...?
✓ What are the differences between ...?
✓ How would you explain to someone else how to ...?
✓ What is wrong with this and how would you correct it?
✓ What evidence can you give for this ...?
✓ Why do you think this is wrong?
✓ Why do you think this is right?
✓ What works well here?
✓ Why is this effective?
✓ What could be improved about this?
✓ How could it be improved?

Approaching exams

As exam time approaches, students can start to experience high levels of stress. This time will probably be especially difficult for your weakest students, who may be used to being judged as failing. It could also be that some of your more able students do not perform to the best of their ability when under the pressure of time in exams.

There are lots of ways in which teachers can help their students approach exams more effectively:

✓ *Give them plenty of practice*: The more exam practice students have, the more comfortable they will feel with the idea of the approaching exam. They should feel that there is no mystery about what is likely to be in the exam, nor about what they need to do, to do well in it.
✓ *Teach them how to revise*: Spend time teaching your students useful revision strategies. Show them techniques for memorizing facts, demonstrate the use of brainstorms for creating revision notes, talk about using time effectively.
✓ *Boost their self-esteem*: Make it clear to your weakest or most nervous students that exams are not the 'be all and end all' in life. Although formal exams are clearly important for their future, you as a teacher

still value them as individuals, whatever grades they achieve in their exams.

✓ *Take advantage of their increased motivation*: As exam time approaches, students generally become much more motivated. They realize that it is important for them to do well, and will tend to work harder in class. Take advantage of this increase in motivation, perhaps by focusing on important coursework, or by getting them to write high-quality pieces for teacher assessment.

Preparing for exams

There is no magical secret to doing well in exams – simply a range of strategies and approaches students can learn. Prepare your students for their written exams by giving them information about what the exam will involve, and also by showing them how to get the best possible results for their level of ability. For some students with special needs, additional help or time may be allowed in the exams. Check with your examinations officer in advance to see if this applies to any of your students.

To prepare your students well for their exams:

✓ Practice, practice, practice: If you teach an 'examination year', exam practice should become a regular part of your classroom routine. There are a number of good reasons for this.

  – With regular practice your students realize that there is little to be scared of in exams.

  – They get used to the general format of the exam paper and start to understand what the examiners want them to do.

  – They learn about timing – how to allocate the correct amount of time to each piece of writing.

  – They can be educated in the way that exams run – the importance of working in complete silence, and not glancing at what their friends are doing.

  – Although exam practice can add to your marking load, you will get a number of 'lessons off' from teacher-led work.

✓ *Plan, plan, plan*: When doing exam practice, there is no need to always write out a full exam answer. A good-quality plan shows you whether or not the student understands how to answer the question. Planning in class also helps your students understand the importance of this part of the writing process, and to practise the skills involved.

✓ *Information is power (1)*: Get your hands on some old exam papers to share with your students. There is nothing more frightening than the unknown – facing an exam paper never having seen a similar one before is confusing for your students. They may waste time trying to understand what the exam paper is asking them to do, time that would be better spent proving their abilities.

✓ *Information is power (2)*: Show your students the marking criteria as well. To gain maximum marks, they need to fulfil these criteria. It is therefore essential that your students understand what they must aim to achieve. For instance, how vital is good technique – accurate spelling, punctuation, etc.? What level of technical language or understanding do they need to demonstrate?

✓ *Show them sample essays*: A good way of demonstrating how to earn the best possible mark is to show your students a sample essay or exam answer. This might be from a high-quality candidate in a previous year's exam, or it could be an essay that you write yourself to show how the question is best answered. You might also ask the students to give a mark for this answer, using the marking criteria.

✓ *Work on sample answers as a whole class*: A good way of approaching exam practice is to split your class into groups, and ask each group to formulate an answer, sharing their ideas with the class. This takes away the pressure of individual work, and allows all the students to contribute their own ideas.

✓ *Show the connection between questions and marks*: Some students fail to understand that a set amount of marks are available for each exam question. Explain to them that:

  – There is no point in writing copious amounts for a question that will only ever earn them two or three marks.
  – Some questions are worth answering in detail, because they offer the chance to earn a high number of marks.
  – If a question has a number of marks available, the students will often be given one mark for each separate point they make on the subject.

✓ *Show the importance of timing*: Exam success has much to do with the ability to time your writing. Self-discipline is required to avoid using up the time available without answering all the questions. Practice under exam conditions will help your students learn about timing. If the exam involves writing long essays, tell your students to write the time that they should finish each essay on the answer booklet. If they run over this time, advise them to start the next essay while leaving space to finish the first one, if they have spare time at the end of the exam.

✓ *Show the importance of the question's phrasing*: Exam questions tend to be phrased in a way that encourages the student to give the correct answer, in the correct form, and referring to the appropriate material. As you spend time going through old papers, take time to look at the language of the questions. Here are some useful discussion points to guide your students:

- Is the question in two or more parts?
- Do the different parts earn you equal marks, or is one part more important than another? Some exam questions look like they only have one part, for instance when they are written in a single paragraph, but are actually asking two separate questions.
- Does the question say something like 'According to the passage what does ...?' If it does, the students must make close reference to the passage in their answer, or use relevant quotations.
- Does the question ask you to use a specific form or layout in your answer?
- What tone should be used for this form?
- Is there a particular viewpoint that is best for answering this question?
- How much detail do you need to give to receive the maximum amount of marks?

Answering exam questions

As well as preparing your students for their exams, you can also help them with writing their answers. Although your more-able students will have worked much of this out for themselves, for others, these strategies are not immediately obvious. Teach your class about these techniques, and how to use them.

Share these ideas with your class:

✓ *Choosing the question*: If the paper gives a choice of questions, talk together about how they might choose the best one to answer. This could involve the student knowing what their individual strengths are, or being clear about what you have studied in class.

✓ *Sticking to the question*: You can find lots of ideas about this in Chapter 6, on essay writing ('Answering the question', p. 102). Reassure your students that they don't need to write down everything they know on a subject. If the material they include doesn't answer the question, they will earn no marks for it.

✓ *Use the question to start your answer*: Many students find it really hard to get started in exams and freeze up, wasting precious minutes.

Encourage them to use the wording of the question to begin their answer, to help them overcome this, and keep themselves 'on track'.

✓ *Keep it simple*: Your more able students might start to over-complicate things in exams, assuming that the answers must be more difficult than they appear to be. Encourage your students to take a step back from the paper, consider carefully what is being asked, then word their answer simply and clearly.

✓ *Don't waffle*: Similarly, some students feel the need to write at great length, when a brief answer would in fact be better. This can cause problems with timing, and it might lose them marks if the examiner feels that they haven't stuck to the question. Encourage students with a tendency to waffle to look closely at the marks available for each answer and write only what is needed to earn those marks.

14

The Writing Clinic

From the errors of others, a wise man corrects his own.

Syrus

This chapter offers a 'writing clinic', in which some of the most common writing problems are explored, through a series of case studies. For each case study, I provide an example of the problem, a diagnosis of why the specific problem is occurring, and strategies for the teacher to use in overcoming the student's particular area of weakness. I have included writing from a range of different ages, to illustrate the problems at different stages in a student's school career.

 You might also like to share the texts below with your students, to explore how to assess writing, or to get them looking at various techniques to make their writing work better. You can find a downloadable version of these texts at the companion website.

Overwriting

> The ripe orange sun bled into the dark blue sea, like a huge orange being squeezed of its juice. A soft, gentle breeze caressed the pure white sand of the beach, which seemed to glow in the last dying gasps of the sun's light. The pretty young girl swept her long curling blonde hair back from her face and sighed deeply, a sad, mournful look on her pale, smooth skinned face.
>
> 'Oh John. How beautiful it is here. What a wonderful day I've had with you. I'm so sad that it has to end.'

Diagnosis

This piece of writing has everything but the kitchen sink! It is melodramatic rather than realistic, and it sounds like something from a romance novel. The writer loves using description and descriptive words, particularly adjectives, and the way that she can make them sound. There are some good moments here, but the language would benefit hugely from watering down. The writer has probably learned about similes and other language devices recently, and is trying to experiment with them. At the moment her experiments are not being terribly successful. She obviously enjoys writing, but has little sense of how her writing comes across to the reader.

Strategies

✓ *Get an overview*: Ask the student to step back from the work and look at its overall effect. Get her to read it out loud to you, then talk together about how it sounds. What would someone reading this story feel?

✓ *Praise the positives*: Highlight the positive aspects of the writing – the idea of an orange being squeezed is creative and interesting, even though it doesn't quite work.

✓ *Experiment with form*: Get the student to try rewriting the piece in a variety of different forms – as a children's story, as a piece of travel writing, as a recipe for the 'perfect holiday beach'.

✓ *Talk about adjectives*: Ask the student to identify all the adjectives within her writing. Now ask her to go through the piece, cutting out all the adjectives. What is the effect of doing this? Can she find another way to put across her descriptions?

✓ *Experiment with similes*: Encourage the student to examine what makes an effective simile. Brainstorm ideas, using a very simple form: 'The sun is like …'

Dull or under-writing

The boy went into the room. There was a table and four chairs in the room. He went over to the chairs and sat down. He waited for the man to arrive. He looked around the room. Then he looked at his watch. He wondered when the man would come.

Diagnosis

This writing is under-written because of the total lack of description. There is a limited use of vocabulary and the writer has not used any connectives. The piece is also dull because nothing of any real interest happens.

Strategies

✓ *Consider the choice of verbs*: Ask the student to look at the verbs he has chosen and try to find a more interesting alternative that suggests something about the boy's character, mood or emotions. He could brainstorm a list of alternatives for each verb. For instance, instead of the verb 'went', the boy might have 'strode', 'stormed', 'raced' or 'crept' into the room. What would these verbs suggest about the boy's character to the reader?

✓ *Consider the use of descriptive language*: Although it's important to avoid an overly descriptive, adjective-laden style, the reader needs some type of detail to be able to visualize what is happening. For instance, when the boy looks around the room, what does he see?

✓ *Use a zoom lens*: Get the student to write a detailed study of one thing inside the room, for instance describing the table in detail. It's useful to equate this to a camera lens, focusing in on a single object. Encourage him to ask himself questions, such as:
  - What material is the table made of?
  - Is it new or old?
  - What colour is it?
  - What size and shape is the table?
  - How does it feel if he rubs his hand over it?
  - Is there anything on the table?

✓ *Consider the development of character*: To give a stronger sense of character, encourage the student to empathize with the character. What is he thinking and feeling? How could this be shown in the way that he moves or the way he reacts to his situation?

✓ *Add some conflict*: Find ways to encourage the student to add conflict and tension to the piece – a problem to be solved, another character with whom to fight, a sense of time running out.

✓ *Use connectives*: Give the student a bank of connectives that he might use, and get him to experiment with adding some of these in. You can find a list of connecting words on the companion website, to share with your class.

Lack of punctuation

Sammy raced out of the door and ran down the street he was late for school and he knew that he would get in trouble when he got to school. when he got to school he sped into the classroom but the teacher had already taken the register and Sammy got into trouble again he hated getting into trouble. why are you late again Sammy the teacher asked I woke up late Sammy said because my alarm didnt go off then you need to mend your alarm the teacher told Sammy. youre in detention with me after school now get on with your work

Diagnosis

This student's writing has a strong sense of pace, but is almost completely lacking in punctuation. I've seen this kind of thing so many times! In a rush to get the ideas down, he has become wrapped up in telling the story rather than thinking about the need to be clear for his reader.

Strategies

✓ *Read it back*: Ask the student to read his work back to you exactly as he has written it. This will help him to see that the reader needs punctuation to show where there is a pause. Now read it again. This time tell the student to pause every time he would naturally take a breath in his reading. Help him put a mark to indicate that this is where the full stops or commas should come.

✓ *Form the sentences*: Encourage your poor punctuator to form each sentence in his head before he writes it down. He can then work on one sentence at a time, adding full stops where necessary.

✓ *Punctuate the dialogue*: The writer has also neglected to punctuate the speech. Ask him to highlight the words in the passage that are actually spoken by a character. Alternatively, he could work through the writing with a partner, and every time someone speaks out loud, his partner could take over. This should help him punctuate the dialogue.

✓ *Offer a punctuation bank*: Look through the piece and count how many full stops, apostrophes, speech marks, etc. are missing. Give your student this many 'credits' at your 'punctuation bank'. You can use small stickers, with punctuation marks written on them, to create your 'credits'.

Repetitive writing

> Jamie climbed up into the cave. Then he took his torch out. Then he shone his torch around the cave. The cave was dark and Jamie couldn't see what was at the back. Then he walked to the back of the cave. When he got to the back of the cave he shone his torch again. When he did this he saw a big spider. When he saw the spider he got very scared. Then he ran out of the cave.

Diagnosis

This writing is very repetitive, and consequently sounds stilted. It is also dull for the reader, because of the lack of interest in the vocabulary. There is excessive use of the word 'then' – a fairly common problem for younger writers who are trying to divide their work up into sentences, and show the chain of events chronologically, but who are not yet using a sufficient variety of adverbs to show the time sequence.

Strategies

✓ *Identify the repetition*: Ask the student to underline any word that is repeated more than two times in the piece of writing. In this case, the words 'cave', 'then' and 'when'. Use a different colour for each repeated word.

✓ *Look for alternatives*: Talk to the student about how a noun such as cave might be replaced by the word 'it'. Alternatively, it is often possible to remove the noun altogether, for instance in the sentence 'Then he shone his torch around the cave.' the words 'the cave' could be completely removed. The sentence would still make sense, as the reader already knows where Jamie is. For each highlighted word, get the student to add in an alternative.

✓ *Develop a bank of sequencing words*: The writer needs to find alternatives to the chain of 'thens' and 'whens'. Use the downloadable connectives sheet, from the companion website, to offer him a bank of words showing a sequence of events: first, next, finally, and so on.

Irrelevant facts

Essay question: *Discuss the characters of Macbeth and Lady Macbeth, exploring the relationship between them, and the way that this relationship changes during the course of the play.*

Shakespeare was born in 1564 in Stratford-upon-Avon. He lived there before moving to London to work as an actor and writer. His play *Macbeth* is about a man called Macbeth who kills the king. The king's name is King Duncan. After he has killed King Duncan, Macbeth himself becomes king. Macbeth's wife is called Lady Macbeth.

Diagnosis

In this example of an essay introduction, the student begins with a list of facts, none of which have any relevance to the question that has been asked. This is typical of the essay writing produced by students who understand the plot of a text, and who have listened to explanations of the historical background. However, there is little awareness here of what is required to answer an essay question, and very limited understanding of theme, character and so on.

Strategies

✓ *Teach the 'four-step' technique*: Use the 'four-step' essay-writing technique described in Chapter 6. This helps the student to understand the steps of explanation and development that are required to write an effective essay, one which will gain them marks in an exam.

✓ *Teach the use of planning brainstorms*: Similarly, this student would benefit from being taught to set out his answer as a series of brainstorms, before beginning to write. You can find details about how to use these, and a set of examples, in Chapter 6.

✓ *Use the question to answer the question*: Encourage the student to start his essay by turning the question into a statement. This will help him stick to the point. In this example, he could write 'The characters Macbeth and Lady Macbeth have a very complex relationship' and then go on to talk about what that relationship is like.

✓ *Assumed knowledge*: Remind the student that he can assume a certain amount of prior knowledge on the part of the person reading the essay. For instance, in this case it is safe to assume that the marker will know the names of the characters and their relationships to each other. Whilst these could be mentioned in passing, there is no need to spell them out in this kind of detail.

Listing

Essay question: *Analyse the imagery used in the poem 'Upon Westminster Bridge' by William Wordsworth.*

In 'Upon Westminster Bridge' Wordsworth uses lots of imagery. He uses lots of personification and similes. He personifies the city, saying that it 'wears' the beauty of the morning. He personifies the river, saying it 'glideth at his own sweet will'. He uses the simile 'like a garment' ...

Diagnosis

The student clearly understands what imagery is, and is keen to show that she can identify examples of personification and similes. However, the problem is that the student does not understand what is meant by the word 'analyse'. Instead she lists the images that she has found, without explaining any of them, or offering any further development of the points. In terms of my 'four-step' essay-writing technique, the student is taking only the first two steps.

Strategies

✓ *Explore the question vocabulary*: Talk to the student about how important it is to examine the vocabulary of the question before trying to write an answer. Ask her to highlight any words that she think might be important, in terms of working out how to write the answer. Here, the word 'analyse' means she is being asked for a detailed examination of the use, effect and purpose of these images.

✓ *Teach steps 3 and 4*: Go over the third and fourth steps of the essay-writing technique with the student (see pp. 109–111). Show her how the explanation and development of a point will gain her the marks. These sentences are where she shows her thinking skills and analytical ideas, rather than just her ability to spot writing techniques.

✓ *Encourage one paragraph per point*: Ask the student to rewrite her essay, giving an entire paragraph to each sentence where she offers an example of imagery. Each paragraph should have four sentences in it, to include an explanation and development of each point.

✓ *Pose the question 'why?'* What's missing here is the student asking herself questions about the writer's use of language. Encourage her to finish every sentence she writes by asking herself the question 'Why does the writer do this?'

15

Celebrating Writing

Don't forget to love yourself.

Kierkegaard

For the weak or the demotivated, writing can seem to be a grind, a daily challenge they must submit themselves to throughout their schooling. This final chapter is about challenging that assumption: about finding ways to celebrate writing, and to make it a joyful and exciting prospect. Although some of the suggestions below will take up quite a lot of your time in preparation and organization, the results in terms of motivation, behaviour and inspiration are more than worth the effort. Many of the ideas below are ones that I have used or been involved in during my teaching career. They stick in my mind as very positive times, and I am certain that the same applies for the students who were involved.

Displaying writing

One of the simplest and quickest ways to celebrate your students' writing is by displaying it for others to read. Seeing their work up on the wall can really motivate your students: essentially, it is being 'published' for the world to see. You can get really creative with your displays, making them interactive, imaginative and inspirational.

Use the ideas below to get you thinking:

✓ *Washing lines*: Hang a line of string or rope across your room, or along a corridor, and peg up examples of your students' work. The great thing about this way of displaying work is that it is easily interchange-able. You can get hold of miniature wooden craft pegs online which work really well for smaller pieces of work.
✓ *The 'working wall'*: This is a display that the students work on and add to, during their lessons. It's not a static, finished display, but a living, growing, interactive one. For instance, for studying *Lord of the Flies* the

teacher draws an outline of the island on the wall. As the students read the book, they add notes to the display – this is where a particular event happened, here's a quote about this part of the island.

✓ *Post box*: Include a post box as part of your display, so that your students can post you their ideas, thoughts or questions. Have a stack of paper and some envelopes beside the post box, and encourage your students to send you a message.

✓ *Interactive features*: The students we teach live in a highly interactive world. Mirror this in your displays by having lift up flaps, questions, a set of sticky notes beside the display for them to add their comments.

✓ *Multi-sensory*: Appeal to all the senses by using different textures. You can even make your displays 'talk' to the viewer, by using recordable talk buttons. Your students can record a short extract of sound on these, which plays back when pressed.

✓ *Three-dimensional*: Create three-dimensional elements within your displays, to give added interest and to encourage the students to interact with them. For instance, you could make the writing jump out by sticking it onto a box, or wrap text around circular shapes.

✓ *What's hiding?* Add some hidden elements in the style of the *Where's Wally* books: for example, a symbol hidden somewhere on the display, with a prize for anyone who finds it. Again, this encourages the students to actually interact with and read the writing that's on display.

✓ *Unusual places*: Have a look around to find unusual places to display work – think laterally to really challenge your students. How about sticking some writing under the desks, and lying on your back to read it? Or writing out some poetry in chalk on the playground for a temporary display?

Add a competitive element to displays as well, by having a space for the 'Writing of the Week'. A great idea I was given is to do this in the style of The X-Factor, with photos and biographies of the top competitors that week.

Publishing writing

For a young writer, seeing their work published is an incredibly motivating experience. For every piece that we write there is an audience, or even a number of audiences. At the simplest level, the audience for the majority of classroom writing is the teacher. Some pieces of writing have a wider audience, for instance those that are put on display, or sent home to parents. The widest audience of all can be found for those pieces of work that are published – either through displays as described above, or through a range of other forms. Here are just a few suggestions for where you can publish your students' writing:

✓ *On the internet*: Writing that is published on the internet has a huge potential audience, right around the world. Seeing a piece of their work published online will motivate your students, and is an excellent way of celebrating writing. You might create your own website or page or use a site that's already up and running. See the companion website for links to sites that publish young people's writing.

✓ *Via a competition*: Setting up a whole-school writing competition, as described below, offers a great way of motivating your students to write, and of publishing the results. Create a booklet of winning entries, for students, staff and parents to read.

✓ *Via a school magazine*: If you are a keen writer and editor yourself, consider setting up a school magazine. I can remember to this day the excitement that was generated by seeing my own work published in a school magazine when I was a child. If the teachers at your school are too busy, see if you can rope in a parent volunteer. I currently run a 'magazine club' at my own children's school, producing a termly magazine to celebrate the children's writing.

✓ *Creating 'books'*: A project in which your students create their own books, from first idea to final product, is an excellent way of celebrating their writing. Of course this would work well for story books, but it could also include books in other areas of the curriculum. These books might be aimed at an audience of younger students within your school, or perhaps a more general audience via the school library. There are also companies that publish books of students' writing, for schools to sell as a fund-raising opportunity. See the companion website for links.

Book weeks

A 'book week' is an excellent way to get the whole school celebrating reading, writing and books in general. Booktrust (www.booktrust.org. uk) organizes an annual book week in the UK, which takes place in the first full week of October. Although a book week might be organized by a literary coordinator in a primary school, or by the English Department in a secondary school, there is no reason why it should not be run in a cross-curricular way – all subjects use books!

During book week, the focus can be on both reading and writing, perhaps with students writing their own books in the style of their favourite authors. You might get local companies to sponsor your school in buying books, or ask local librarians to come in with a selection of books from the libraries in your area.

Author days/weeks

A day or week dedicated to one author is a great opportunity to get your students reading and writing in earnest. For instance, in one school my English Department organized a Shakespeare Day. Many of the teachers dressed up as characters from the plays, and we performed scenes to the students. The children were involved in different writing activities, including creating Shakespearean love poems. By raising the profile of an author in this way, you also raise the profile of writers and books in general. There is no need, of course, to stick to writers from the past. For instance, a *Harry Potter* day or week would go down extremely well too.

Charity activities

Children love the chance to 'make a difference', to raise money for a cause that is close to their hearts. Many schools already take part in Red Nose Day or the Children in Need appeal. When developing charity activities for these times, consider the role that writing might play. For instance, there could be a sponsored write as well as the more typical sponsored read. The students could 'set lines' for their teachers, and sponsor them for writing out their lines 100 or 1,000 times.

Competitions

Capitalize on the competitive streak that seems to run through many young people. In one school where I worked, I set up a poetry competition to encourage writing. I was inundated with entries, and the winning and highly commended entries were published in a booklet. This was sold to students, parents and staff to help fund the printing costs and the prizes of book tokens. Competitions can be in subjects other than English, for instance a science competition for the best design and instructions for building a space rocket.

Writers' workshops

There are many professional writers who provide workshops for schools. These might be about storytelling, poetry, writing from other cultures, and so on. Having an 'expert' come in from outside the school is very good for motivating your students with their own writing. You'll pick up fresh ideas and inspiration and new ways of working. For links to find writers to visit your school, see the companion website.

'Play in a day'

It's a wonderful experience to write alongside your students, and one great way of doing this is to organize a 'Play in a day'. This could take place at the end of term, when the whole school is off timetable, for instance on an activity day. Alternatively, this could happen on a day when your school holds a 'break out' or 'collapse' day (a day when the normal timetable is collapsed, and a variety of creative cross-curricular projects take place).

The basic format of the 'Play in a day' is exactly as it sounds: the teacher and students work together to produce a play in only one day, using a specified theme or the outline of a story. They then present this play to the rest of the school at the end of the day, or perhaps on the last day of term. The great thing about this exercise is that most of the 'writing' takes place through improvization, and it is therefore very suitable for students who struggle with putting their thoughts down on paper.

Trips

Trips and visits offer a great way of inspiring good writing. The students are visiting new places, seeing new things, and will actually want to make a written record of their trip after the event. For instance, you might take your class to a local festival, and this could inspire some descriptive writing about what they have seen. You could take them to a museum and ask them to write about one of the exhibits. You could take them to a nearby National Trust property, or an arboretum. For many children, a trip is one of the most memorable and exciting events in their school career.

Part 5

Resources for Writing

Appendix 1

Text messaging

If we want to motivate our students to write, the activities we set must be topical and fun: and what could be more topical than text messaging? Here is a list of some of the more common text-message abbreviations. Many of these terms are simply the shortest possible phonic abbreviations, often using numbers such as 4 and 8 for their sounds. Alternatively, some use acronyms to replace commonly used phrases.

All the best	ATB
Are	R
Are you OK	RUOK?
Be	B
Before	B4
Be seeing you	BCNU
Bye bye for now	BB4N
Cutie	QT
Date	D8
Easy	EZ
Excellent	XLNT
For	4
For your information	FYI
Great	GR8
If you know what I mean	IFKWIM
In my opinion	IMO
Later	L8R
Laugh out loud	LOL
Oh I see	OIC
Please call me	PCM
Roll on the floor laughing	ROFL
See you later	CU L8R

Appendix 1: Text Messaging

Thanks	THX
To/too	2
Today	2DAY
Tomorrow	2MORO
Tonight	2NITE
Want to	WAN2
Why	Y
You	U

For a full list of abbreviations, go here: www.txtdrop.com/abbreviations. php

Appendix 2

Useful websites

The list below details a range of sites dealing with the written word. As far as possible, I have tried to use websites that have been running for a while, or ones backed by large organizations, which are likely to remain online. I have tried to weed out the sites that subject you to those irritating pop-up adverts, or that are overly commercial. You can find a longer list of links at the companion website.

General

www.nationalstrategies.standards.dcsf.gov.uk/
The National Strategies website.

www.nate.org.uk
The website of the National Association for the Teaching of English.

www.everybodywrites.org.uk
A project run by Booktrust and The National Literacy Trust.

Writing resources

www.oxforddictionaries.com
The website of the Oxford Dictionaries.

www.edufind.com/english/grammar
A useful directory of grammatical activities and resources.

www.word-detective.com
A site about the origin and meaning of words.

www.bl.uk
A website of the British Library, with a section devoted to language and literature.

www.wordpool.co.uk
A useful website with lots of writing-related resources.

Teaching resources

www.teachit.co.uk
A free library of English resources, useful for secondary teachers.

www.teachingideas.co.uk
An excellent resource with lots of ideas for teaching English at primary school level.

www.teachingtips.co.uk
A site for secondary teachers, run by Longman Pearson.

Story writing

www.ministryofstories.org
The 'Ministry of Stories', an organization set up to inspire story writing.

Children's books and authors

www.booktrust.org.uk
The site of the Book Trust, which runs the National Children's book week.

www.ncll.org.uk
The site of the National Centre for Language and Literacy. This site has an author database where you can search for an author willing to visit your school.

Special educational needs

www.dyslexia-inst.org.uk
The website of the Dyslexia Institute.

www.bdadyslexia.org.uk
The website of the British Dyslexia Association.

Appendix 3

Vocabulary

The lists below gives useful vocabulary for written work. You might like to use these to introduce key terms, or to set spelling tests for your students. I have included a list of some of the most commonly used words, which are useful for teaching and consolidating important vocabulary. I have also included a list of words that, in my experience, cause particular problems for students. For downloadable copies of these lists, and subject specific vocabulary lists, see the companion website.

Commonly used words

a, about, across, after, again, all, almost, among, an, and, any, as, at, be, because, before, between, by, come, do, down, enough, even, ever, every, far, for, forward, from, get, give, go, have, he, hear, here, how, I, if, in, keep, let, little, make, may, me, much, near, no, not, now, of, off, on, only, or, other, our, out, over, please, put, quite, said, say, see, seem, send, she, so, some, still, such, take, than, that, the, then, there, this, though, through, to, together, tomorrow, under, up, very, well, when, where, while, who, why, will, with, yes, yesterday, you, your

Commonly used nouns

ant, apple, arm, baby, bag, ball, band, basket, bath, bed, bee, bell, bird, board, boat, book, boot, bottle, box, boy, branch, brick, bridge, brush, bucket, button, cake, camera, card, cart, cat, chain, cheese, chin, church, circle, clock, cloud, coat, collar, cow, cup, curtain, cushion, dog, door, drawer, dress, ear, egg, engine, eye, face, farm, feather, finger, fish, flag, floor, fly, foot, fork, garden, girl, glove, hair, hand, hat, head, heart, horse, hospital, house, island, jewel, kettle, key, knee, knife, leaf, leg, library, line, lip, lock, map, match, monkey, moon, mouth, nail, neck, needle, net, nose, nut, office, orange, oven, parcel, pen, pencil, picture, pig, pin, plane, plate, pocket, pot, potato, rail, rat, ring, roof, root, sail, school, scissors, sheep, shelf, ship, shirt, shoe, skirt, snake, sock, spade, spoon, square, stamp, star, station, stick, stomach, street, sun, table, tail, thumb, ticket, toe, tooth, town, train, tree, trousers, umbrella, wall, watch, wheel, window, wing, worm

Problem words for older students

accommodation, beautiful, beginning, cautious, competition, definitely, desperate, disguise, exaggerate, explanation, extraordinary, February, frightened, laughter, occasion, opinion, particularly, patiently, prejudice, privilege, separate, successfully, suspicious

Commonly misspelled words

affect, benefited, calendar, concede, discrete, grievance, innovative, occurred, practise, principle, truly, withhold

English

Linguistic analysis

alliteration, atmosphere, cliché, comparison, expression, figurative, imagery, metaphor, onomatopoeia, personification, simile

Spelling, punctuation and grammar

apostrophe, clause, comma, conjunction, consonant, exclamation, homonym, paragraph, plural, prefix, preposition, subordinate, suffix, synonym, vocabulary, vowel

Writing about texts

advertise, advertisement, chorus, climax, dialogue, genre, myth, narrative, narrator, opinion, pamphlet, playwright, rehearse, resolution, rhyme, scene, significant, soliloquy, tabloid

Writing about characters

ambitious, cautious, character, characterization, courageous, despised, disguise, enemies, foolish, hypocritical, notorious, obedient, rebellious, relationship, serious, vicious

Letter writing

apologize, complain, enquire, faithfully, forward, information, madam, receive, sincerely, writing

Appendix 4

Marking symbols

The marking symbols below should make marking your students' written work quicker, simpler and more effective. Encourage your students to use these symbols too, either when they're editing their own writing, or when they're marking someone else's. It's a great idea to get your students to put a set of the agreed marking symbols in the front of their exercise books, to refer back to. The boxed symbols below can be photocopied for your own personal use with your students.

~~	Expression/grammar/vocabulary needs amending
_____	Spelling mistake/word is wrong
/	New line needed here
//	New paragraph needed here
^	Word missing/insert word or letter
O	Punctuation missing
?	Unclear/I don't understand what is meant
/	Cut letter/punctuation
v	Good section
vv	Excellent section
[ ]	This section needs redrafting
↗	Move that bit to here

Index

Index

Index